Willard R. Espy

Illustrations by Charles C. Hefling, Jr.

HAVE A WORD ON ME

A Celebration of Language

Simon and Schuster

New York

PUBLISHED BY SIMON AND SCHUSTER
A DIVISION OF GULF & WESTERN CORPORATION
SIMON & SCHUSTER BUILDING
ROCKEFELLER CENTER
1230 AVENUE OF THE AMERICAS
NEW YORK, NEW YORK 10020
SIMON AND SCHUSTER AND COLOPHON ARE TRADEMARKS OF
SIMON & SCHUSTER

FIVE CHAPTERS OF THIS BOOK ORIGINALLY APPEARED, IN A SLIGHTLY DIFFERENT
FORM, AS ARTICLES IN *Harvard Magazine* AND ONE AS AN ARTICLE IN *Games*

DESIGNED BY ELIZABETH WOLL

MANUFACTURED IN THE UNITED STATES OF AMERICA

1   3   5   7   9   10   8   6   4   2

LIBRARY OF CONGRESS CATALOGING IN PUBLICATION DATA

ESPY, WILLARD R.
HAVE A WORD ON ME
"FIVE CHAPTERS OF THIS BOOK ORIGINALLY APPEARED, IN A SLIGHTLY
DIFFERENT FORM, AS ARTICLES IN HARVARD MAGAZINE."—VERSO T.P.
1. ENGLISH LANGUAGE—ETYMOLOGY.   2. ENGLISH LANGUAGE
—ANECDOTES, FACETIAE, SATIRE, ETC.   I. TITLE.
PE1574.E8   422   81-1363
AACR2

ISBN 0-671-25255-0

Contents

Preface

RELATED here, more or less in the order in which they came to mind, are some speculations and opinions about where language came from and where it is going. With little rhyme or reason I have interspersed reflections on rhyme and reason, and such other irrelevancies as the story of the origin of the King James Version of the Holy Bible.

Only the unwary will enter *The House of Words* in search of knowledge. Such information as may emerge is here by accident, a by-product of my pleasure in the oddities of word origins and usage. Where I cite an example of a point that interests me, I hope you will be able to add ten or a hundred—or cite evidence for a different theory altogether.

At times I have quoted from the recorded remarks of such distinguished visitors from the past as Dr. Johnson and Lewis Carroll. But I have also put into their mouths words and opinions which they would doubtless disavow if they were around to do so. My apologies to their shades. I was impressed, incidentally, by their familiarity with language changes that took place after their deaths; clearly, someone keeps the reference libraries in Eternity up to date.

Several chapters of this book first appeared in slightly different form as magazine articles, and I am grateful for permission to reprint them. I owe deep gratitude, too, to Timothy Dickinson, who brought to my attention most of the etymological oddities you will read about here; his supply of erudition is frightening. I am indebted to Christopher Gray for many good services in support of the book. My wife, Louise, helped me close in on what I was trying to say; indeed, she made the whole exercise possible. Fred Hills and Catherine Shaw exceeded the call of editorial duty in suggesting ways to rub out some of the roughness and to give *The House of Words* the semblance of an organic whole.

WILLARD R. ESPY

Introduction

ACQUAINTANCES have been known to describe me in Shakespearean terms: "Not so much brain as beeswax."

But they are dead wrong. Faded papers and broken-down chairs may be heaped in my mental attic; but beeswax? No. Those scribblings may yet fuel a fire to warm someone's chilled toes. Those wobbly chairs may yet go for a pretty penny at Sotheby Parke Bernet.

To be sure, my brain is unlike theirs, or yours, which are the enlarged and greatly modified portion of the cerebrospinal nervous axis contained within the cranium. Your axis consists of the forebrain, the interbrain, the midbrain, and two or three attachments farther back. One of these is the nose-brain—I suppose, like noses on the exterior of the head, pugged, hooked, or aquiline, according to inheritance. If you are a grown male, your brain weighs about fifty ounces; if a female, about forty-four. Congress, however, has under consideration a constitutional amendment to prohibit a comparison of male and female brains by weight or in any other way; by the time you read these words, we may have struck one more overdue blow against sexual discrimination.

My own brain, on the other hand, is not in my head at all—a statement that will come as no surprise to those who know me best. Instead, it spends most of its time in an otherwise unoccupied four-story house of flaking brownstone at 479 East Fifty-first Street, Manhattan. I pass the house frequently on the way to lunch at my club, but have entered it physically only once, in the spring of 1962, when my wife and I were casting about for quarters sizable enough to accommodate her children, my children, and perhaps someday our children. We were thinking of buying a house, renovating it, and renting the ground floor to a business concern at a rate sufficient to cover taxes and upkeep.

The notion proved impractical, but during our exploration of the building I made an odd discovery. A framed, glass-covered sampler had been left hanging on a bedroom wall. I rubbed away the dust that had made the glass opaque, and read a message woven in the uneven stitches of a child's hand. It went like this:

> Though Brain with me may disagree
>   On who retains the Tether,
>   The matter's moot.
> We're linked as Dryad to her tree;
>   And when the Ax shall lop our root,
>   We'll fall together.

Not only was it a curious theme for a child's sampler, but the verse left me with a feeling of *déjà vu*. And rightly so; when I checked my files at home, I found I had written it myself.

It was not until December 11, 1970, my birthday, that my connection with the house was made clear. In celebration of the event, some hundred and fifty well-wishers had crowded into our apartment, where, had it been licensed, any number over fifty would surely have been illegal. When the last guest had departed I sat awhile at my study desk, abrim with alcohol and sentiment, yet vaguely anticipatory: the evening seemed incomplete. My thoughts wandered; I found myself walking up the steps of 479 East Fifty-first Street, drifting through the heavy oak of the door, and entering my own brain.

The few intimates to whom I have described this experience tend to shrug off the house on Fifty-first Street as a figment. It is not. You can go and see it for yourself, from the outside.* Of all living creatures, however, only I can enter and leave it at will, unperceived.

The left brain is supposed to control the right side of the body and notions associated with writing, logic, memory, and the like, while the right brain entertains creative or intuitive concepts. But the house on Fifty-first Street fits neither of these distinctions. Certainly it is not the humdrum affair associated with the left brain; nor can it be simply the right, supposedly a verbal idiot, for it is above all a house of words.

I have concluded that my right brain got me into the house, but that my left brain lives there. In practice, this means that on my frequent visits to the house on Fifty-first Street I proceed directly to the library and settle down to browse through books.

The library is an elegant, inviting space—largeish, square, with a high molded ceiling (the design a wreath of flowers surrounding a pink cupid) from the center of which is suspended an elaborate crystal chandelier.

The south wall is broken by two large windows of many small panes, facing Fifty-first Street but, like magical prisms, conjuring up images at will. The side walls are lined floor to ceiling with books. Centered in the west wall, to which my desk sits at right angles, is a large Georgian fireplace, in which I usually have logs ablaze. It is surmounted by a Blakelock painting of a full moon shining on water; when the lights are out, I can still see the moon shining and its luminescence in the water.

The library, like the rest of the house's interior, is the

* The situation has changed since I wrote this, as you will see on page 255.

creation of my mind; a thought would change it in any way I might wish. But I like it as is. The furniture consists, besides my desk, of two low, soft couches facing each other at right angles to the windowed wall; a coffee table between them; a bar near the fireplace; scatterings of straight or soft chairs of the middle Victorian period; and, in the middle of the room, in a mahogany holder, a five-foot globe that changes its names and boundary lines to fit any date I may happen to be checking.

Sometimes, when my mind is on them, the authors of the books come to call.

MESSAGE FOUND TIED TO
THE NECK OF A DROWNED DOVE

Off, book, to Ararat; and from that peak
    Bring olive leaf for token, wanting words.
    Fly right this time; I'm sick of how you birds
Keep limping home with brick-bats in your beak.

I go into the grounds, the extended mansions of remembrance, where is stored the endless import of my senses. There, too, is record kept of thoughts added to the sensual imprints, or subtracted from them, or varying them in combination. Indeed, everything ever committed to remembrance is still laid up there, unless long decayed or sunk beyond retrieval. On visits there I make request for what I would withdraw, and some are issued instantly, while others must be sought for at some length in deeper vaults. Still others, clamorous, pour out unbidden, and while a different thing was asked for and is being sought, they dance, as it were, before me, saying, "Wasn't it us you were wanting?" And I banish them, with a hand's brush of the heart, from the presence of my memory, until what I seek is brought from its cobwebs and restored to light.

ST. AUGUSTINE, *The Confessions*

1

HAPPY BIRTHDAY, BOSH AND BLURB!

I WAS writing down a list of words with known birth-days, or at least known birthyears. Why was I spending my time so pointlessly when I might just as easily have been taking a nap? Sir or Madam, I am a man of iron discipline, and my nap was not due for another half-hour.

I had just written down two words that ended in -*ation*. Why only two, you ask, when there are words by the thousands with the same ending? As it happens, all the others arrived in English from Romance languages, with the -*ation* already attached: "concentration," "hal-lucination," "imagination," and so on. But my two, and to the best of my knowledge those two only, were good old English words onto which someone had deliberately grafted -*ation* as a suffix.

The earlier of the two was "flirt." The actor and poet Colley Cibber decided to pretty it up. "You know," he wrote, "I always loved a little flirt*ation*." That was in the year 1718; "flirtation" was soon as popular a word as the activity it described.

Fifty-seven years passed before -*ation* was added to another English word. In 1775, during a debate in Parliament on a bill "for restraining Trade and Commerce with the New England Colonies," an M.P. named Henry Dundas expressed doubt that the bill would be strong enough to produce the famine at which it aimed. Opposition speakers added -*ation* to "starve," excoriating him as "starvation Dundas."

I had just finished noting, " 'flirtation'—1718; 'starvation'—1775" when two fat little men, clearly twins, came through the door, walking very carefully sidewise, for they were carrying between them a china platter which held a white coconut-covered cake four layers high. They set it on the table and began adjusting its position, saying in low, intense tones, "More to the right!"—"Contrariwise, more to the left!"—"Nohow!" and so on, until it was exactly centered. Then they stood back to admire it.

"I am to put in the candles," said Tweedledum. (The twins were identical in appearance, but their names were embroidered on their collars.)

"Contrariwise, we are both to put in the candles," said Tweedledee.

"But I am to light them."

"Contrariwise, we are to take turns lighting them."

"But we both are to blow them out."

"Nohow—*he* is to blow them out," said Tweedledee, pointing over his shoulder.

I looked where he was pointing, and was delighted to recognize Lewis Carroll standing before the fireplace. He was a thin, very erect old man, clean-shaven and with a shy smile; he had set his tall hat on the mantelpiece; he wore clerical coat and turned-down collar, with a rumpled white tie.

He spoke with a hesitation in his gentle voice that might have been due either to shyness or to a speech impediment. "I have been told," he said, "that your house is Liberty Hall for words. Perhaps you would join us in a little birthday celebration."

"Gladly," I said. "Whose birthday?"

"Not yours!" said Tweedledum.

"Nohow!" said Tweedledee.

"The birthday party is for the words I coined in *Jabberwocky*," said Carroll.

"Would that have been in 1872," I inquired, "when *Through the Looking Glass* came out?"

"No—much earlier. I wrote *Jabberwocky* in 1855. It lay around in manuscript form for seventeen years."

"Unbirthday words aren't invited," said Tweedledum.

"Nohow," said Tweedledee.

"It would be a great treat for me," I said, "if you would recite *Jabberwocky* for me, Mr. Carroll." (Here I paused a moment in embarrassment, thinking he might be offended at being addressed by his pen name, when his real name was Charles Lutwidge Dodgson; but he only smiled and nodded, so I continued:) "It is not often that I have a chance to hear a great poem recited by its author, especially one of your generation."

"With pleasure," he said, and began at once, his hands hanging loosely at his sides, his voice growing firmer:

> 'Twas brillig, and the slithy toves
>   Did gyre and gimble in the wabe;
> All mimsy were the borogoves,
>   And the mome raths outgrabe.
>
> "Beware the Jabberwock, my son!
>   The jaws that bite, the claws that catch!
> Beware the Jubjub bird, and shun
>   The frumious Bandersnatch!"
>
> He took his vorpal sword in hand;
>   Long time the manxome foe he sought.—
> So rested he by the Tumtum tree,
>   And stood awhile in thought.
>
> And as in uffish thought he stood,
>   The Jabberwock, with eyes of flame,

Came whiffling through the tulgey wood,
        And burbled as it came!

One, two! One, two! And through and through
        The vorpal blade went snicker-snack!
He left it dead, and with its head
        He went galumphing back.

"And hast thou slain the Jabberwock?
        Come to my arms, my beamish boy!
O frabjous day! Callooh! Callay!"
        He chortled in his joy.

'Twas brillig, and the slithy toves
        Did gyre and gimble in the wabe;
All mimsy were the borogoves,
        And the mome raths outgrabe.

"Did you know," I inquired after thanking him, "that
two of your *Jabberwocky* coinages are now accepted in
the *Oxford English Dictionary?*"
    "How nice! Do you remember which?"
    "First, 'chortle'—"
    "A portmanteau word," said Carroll—" 'chuckle'
combined with 'snort.' "
    "Happy birthday, Chortle!" shouted the twins.
Tweedledum set a blue candle in the cake, and Tweedledee lighted it with a kitchen match.
    "The second word is 'galumph.' "
    "Another portmanteau word, combining 'gallop' and
'triumph.' "
    I joined the twins in crying, "Happy birthday, Ga-
lumph!" This time the candle was pink.
    "Would you mind if I threw in some other birthday
words I have found?" I asked, warming to the occasion.
    "We would," said Tweedledum.
    "Would mind, that is," said Tweedledee.

"We would be delighted," said Carroll. "Why don't you start with one of your words, and we'll take turns?"

" 'Blatant' is my first, then," I said. "Fifteen ninety-two. It was coined by Spenser in the twelfth canto of the fifth book of *The Faerie Queen*."

" 'The Blatant Beast,' " quoted Carroll, "has a hundred tongues and a sting. With his tongue, he speaks things 'most shameful, most unrighteous, most untrue. With his sting he steeps words in poison.' A fiend indeed."

"Yet Spenser seems simply to have borrowed 'blatant' from an odd word meaning to bleat, like a sheep, or at most to bellow, like a bull," I said.

"Happy birthday, Blatant!" we shouted (Lewis Carroll excepted) as Tweedledee lighted a yellow candle.

"I shall take the *Jabberwocky* words in order," said Carroll. "I have left instructions," he continued, "that in the first verse the 'i' in 'slithy' is long, as in 'writhe'; 'toves' is pronounced so as to rhyme with 'groves'; and the first 'o' in 'borogoves' is pronounced like the 'o' in 'borrow.' "

"Your first coined word in *Jabberwocky*," I said, "was 'brillig.' "

"Yes. As Humpty Dumpty said, 'brillig' means four o'clock in the afternoon—the time when you begin *broiling* things for dinner."

"Happy birthday, Brillig!" came the chorus.

"My turn," I said. " 'Panjandrum.' Seventeen fifty-five. Samuel Foote invented the word in a nonsense paragraph to test the memory of the actor Macklin, who claimed to be able to memorize any passage at a reading."

"The paragraph went like this," said Carroll:

> So she went into the garden to cut a cabbage-leaf
> to make an apple pie, and at the same time a great
> she-bear came running up the street and popped

its head into the shop. "What! No soap?" So he died, and she—very imprudently—married the barber. And there were present the Picninnies, the Joblillies, the Garyulies, and the Grand Panjandrum himself, with the little red button at top, and they all fell to playing the game of catch-as-catch-can till the gunpowder ran out at the heels of their boots.

"Macklin," I said, "was so furious that he refused to recite the lines."

"Happy birthday, Panjandrum!"

"The last word in the first line of *Jabberwocky* is 'toves,' " said Carroll. "Humpty Dumpty said toves are something like badgers—something like lizards—something like cork-screws. They make their nests under sun-dials, and live on cheese."

"I am afraid that toves can never flourish outside the land of *Jabberwocky*," I said. "Still, lads—all together, now—"

"Happy birthday, Toves!"

"My next," I said, "is 'tomcat.' Seventeen sixty. Until that year, the male of the cat was known as a gib, shortened from 'Gilbert'; but in 1760 a popular tale was published entitled *The Life and Adventures of a Cat,* with Tom the Cat as its hero. Tom proved so irresistible that 'gibs' disappeared from language about cats, except in occasional reference to altered males; all other males are now toms."

More birthday salutes; another blazing candle. "Shall we warm the festivities," I said, "by toasting our birthday words in wine?"

"Do so, by all means," said Carroll. "But I fear I must refrain; I am very nearly a teetotaller. *There* is a birthday word for you. It was first used in England in 1833 in a talk by Richard Turner, of Preston, Lancashire, advocating abstinence not just from ardent spirits but from all intoxicating liquors, including beer. Do you suppose the initial 't' stands for 'tea'?"

Our next toast was to the Jabberwockian coinage "gimble"—"to make holes like a gimlet." I said then, to the usual salutes:

"I give you 'gerrymander.' Eighteen twelve. Elbridge Gerry was Governor of Massachusetts, and the map of the Commonwealth had been redistricted so as to secure disproportionate representation of one political party over another. Gilbert Stuart, the artist, visiting an editor named Benjamin Russell, was inspired by the map of one district pasted to the wall to draw in head, wings, and claws, exclaiming, 'That will do for a salamander!' '*Gerry*mander, rather!' retorted the editor; and 'gerrymander' entered political language as a word meaning manipulation of district lines for political advantage."

Carroll countered with "wabe."

"Alice speculated, quite rightly," he said, "that a wabe is the grass-plot around a sun-dial; it goes a long waybe-*fore* the sun-dial, and a long waybe-*hind* it, and a long waybe-*yond* it on each side."

"Happy birthday, Waybe, baby!" cried Tweedledum and Tweedledee in a persistent chorus that continued throughout the evening, accompanied by the lighting of candles and my ceremonial sips of wine.

" 'Tabloid,' " I offered. "An exact birthday this time —March 14, 1884, when the firm of Messrs. Burroughs, Wellcome & Company trademarked the term for a condensed medical tablet. Because of the small size of the pills, 'tabloid' was soon used to describe newspapers of small dimensions, generally sensational in their approach to the events of the day."

The birthday cake was beginning to twinkle like a Christmas tree.

" 'Mimsy,' " said Carroll. "It combines 'flimsy' and 'miserable.' "

" 'Subway.' Eighteen twenty-eight. Coined by John

Williams, of Cornhill, to describe a system he proposed of underground utility piping."

The words winged back and forth, with greetings ringing in the air and the level of my wine dropping steadily in the bottle.

Carroll: " 'Borogove.' Humpty Dumpty described it as a thin, shabby-looking bird with its feathers sticking out all around—something like a live mop."

Espy: "The borogove too, I fear, will live out its life confined to the bestiary of *Jabberwocky*. I present 'bosh.' Eighteen thirty-four. The word was Turkish, meaning 'empty, worthless'; but in that year James Justinian Morier used it so frequently in his novel *Ayesha* that we have been going around saying 'bosh' in English ever since."

Carroll: " 'Mome raths.' 'Rath' is a sort of green pig. 'Mome' is short for 'from home,' meaning that the pigs had lost their way."

Espy: " 'Golliwog.' Eighteen ninety-five. A kind of bogeyman, taking its name from the black doll designed that year by Florence Upton for the Golliwog Series, written by her sister Bertha. The word was perhaps suggested by 'polliwog.' "

Carroll: " 'Frumious.' An admixture of 'fuming' and 'furious.' I repeat what I said years ago: make up your mind that you will say both words, but leave it unsettled which you will say first. Now open your mouth and speak. If your thoughts incline ever so little towards 'fuming,' you will say 'fuming-furious'; if they turn, by even a hair's breadth, towards 'furious,' you will say 'furious-fuming'; but if you have that rarest of gifts, a perfectly balanced mind, you will say 'frumious.' "

Espy: "There is an almost exact birthday for 'smog.' On July 3, 1905, the *London Globe* wrote: 'The other day at a meeting of the Public Health Congress Dr. Des Boeux did a public service in coining a new word for the London fog, which he referred to as 'smog,' a compound of 'smoke' and 'fog.' "

Carroll: " 'Vorpal,' from the third stanza of *Jabberwocky*. Might it have united 'voracious' and 'corporal'? I no longer have the least idea."

Espy: " 'Bromide' and 'blurb.' Nineteen seven. In that year Gelett Burgess brought out *Are You a Bromide?*, which had a dust jacket embellished with a drawing of a sickly young woman named Miss Belinda Blurb. A 'bromide' is a trite remark, while 'blurb' came to mean inflated publicity, like the exaggerated praise frequently found on a book jacket."

(The birthday cake was coming to resemble a fireworks display.)

Carroll: " 'Manxome,' also from my third stanza. It mixes 'handsome,' 'monstrous,' and a Manx cat."

Espy: " 'Googol.' About 1935, Edward Kasner, the mathematician, asked his nine-year-old nephew to supply a term for the number 10 raised to the power 100. 'Googol,' replied the nephew; and the word was enshrined in the mathematical lexicon."

Carroll: " 'Uffish.' From the first line of my fourth stanza: 'And, as in uffish thought he stood.' 'Uffish' means a bit uppish, but also a bit huffy."

I said, " 'Fifth column.' Nineteen thirty-six. The words are not new, but the sense is. Spanish Rebel General Emilio Mola declared he had four columns of troops outside besieged Madrid and another column hiding in the city ready to join the invaders as soon as they entered the capital. 'Fifth column' ever since has described a clandestine organization working within a country to further the objectives of an invading enemy."

"The 'whiffling' of the Jabberwock is self-explanatory," said Carroll; " 'whiffling' is heavy breathing."

Espy: " 'Middlebrow.' Nineteen forty-nine. Coined by Russell Lynes to signify a person of middling culture, somewhere between highbrow and lowbrow. In 1965 Dwight Macdonald first used 'mid-cult' as an intermediate level of culture, adding 'mass-cult' for the state underneath."

Carroll: "It was through the 'tulgey' wood that the Jabberwock came whiffling. Perhaps I was mixing 'thick' with 'bulging,' though I don't know why. The Jabberwock also 'burbled.' 'Gurgle' and 'bubble,' that is, stirred in together."

Espy: " 'Egghead.' Nineteen fifty-two. Adlai Stevenson, regarded as a man of the mind, ran for the United States Presidency. His head being bald and somewhat egg-shaped, 'egghead' became a generally derogatory term for those of the intellectual persuasion."

"I'll pass Stanza Five of *Jabberwocky*," said Carroll. "We've discussed 'vorpal' and 'galumphing' already, and 'snicker-snack' is only an in-and-out thrust of a weapon."

"I give you 'gung-ho,' " I said. "Nineteen thirty-nine. General E. Carson borrowed this Pidgin expression—perhaps a combination of Mandarin Chinese *kun*, 'work,' plus *ho*, 'together'—as a slogan for the spirit of the Marines. If you are enthusiastic, perhaps overenthusiastic, about participation in a difficult project, you are gung-ho."

"The climax of *Jabberwocky* arrives in Stanza Six," said Carroll, "but most of the new words there are merely variants rather than coinages—'beamish'; 'callooh'; 'callay.' 'Frabjous' is 'frantically, biliously joyous.' "

" 'Mumpsimus,' " I responded. "Fifteen seventeen. Meaning obstinate adherence to old ways. Richard Pace wrote an account of an illiterate priest who regularly read *'mumpsimus'* in the postcommunion of the Mass for *'sumpsimus'*—*'quod in ore sumpsimus':* 'what we have taken in our mouth.' When corrected, the priest is said to have replied, 'I will not change my old *'mumpsimus'* for your new *'sumpsimus.'* "

"I shall go beyond *Jabberwocky* to add two words to my birthday list," said Carroll. "One day in 1874, at Guilford, there appeared in my mind the line 'For the snark *was* a boojum, you see.' ('Snark' merges 'snark' and 'shark.') From that one line I developed the entire story of *The Hunting of the Snark*. To this day I cannot picture either a snark or a boojum clearly. But enough of my own words. I can give you words other than mine with fairly sure birthdays, if you are interested."

I was.

"One is 'Philistine,' in its present sense as a person lacking all culture. It dates from 1683, when a university student at Jena, Saxony, was killed in a riot between town and gown. The funeral speaker took his text from Judges: 'The Philistines be upon thee, Samson.' University students everywhere began calling the townspeople Philistines, and the word came to denote cultural barbarians in general."

"On June 16, 1900," I said, "the verb 'to stellenbosch' was added to the language. It means to demote someone to an innocuous post as a result of his incompetence. Stellenbosch, part of the Cape Colony, was formerly selected as the place of command for officers who had failed in the Kaffir Wars. Rudyard Kipling first used the word in its present sense when he wrote in the *Daily Express:* 'After all, what does it matter, old man? You're bound to be Stellenbosched in three days.' "

"A word that changed its primary meaning in a certain year is 'castaway,' " said Carroll. "It first meant a reprobate, one cast off by God, as in I Corinthians: 'lest that by any means, when I have preached to others, I myself should be a castaway.' But in 1799 William Cowper wrote a poem about a shipwrecked sailor, *The Castaway,* giving the word its present sense as 'a derelict of the sea.' "

I said (my speech was beginning to blur), " 'Doctrinaire' was coined in 1814 to describe a body of French politicians who were working for a limited constitutional monarchy. They opposed both an absolute monarchy and a republic. The two extremes considered them impractical theorizers, frozen to a doctrine, and labeled them 'doctrinaire' when actually they were far more flexible than either the far right or the far left."

"The word 'shark' has a birthday," said Carroll. "In 1569 the sailors of Captain John Hawkins' expedition brought one of the dreadful fishes home. The sailors gave it its name because of its rapacity and possibly from an association of ideas with 'sharp' for a sharper."

By this time the wine had so raised my spirits that I found myself shouting, "Happy birthday!" at random. I remember bellowing that the birthday of 'quark,' a word adopted by both physicists and astronomers, was May 4, 1939, when it appeared in James Joyce's *Finnegans* [sic] *Wake:* "Three quarks for Mr. Marks." And I insisted that the nonsense expression 'supercalifragilisticexpialidocious' was not, as claimed, created in 1964 for the Walt Disney motion picture *Mary Poppins;* a correspondent, I said, had reported hearing it from his teacher as early as 1926.

Without warning the birthday cake burst into flames. Tweedledum and Tweedledee scurried about, trying to extinguish it with bolsters, hearth rugs, tablecloths, dishcovers, and coal scuttles, and I threw a tea tray on top of what was quickly becoming a bonfire. By the time the fire was finally out I had managed to eat several chunks of the cake, and Lewis Carroll had slipped away.

After that I joined Tweedledum and Tweedledee in singing *Jabberwocky,* and continued solo as they staggered out the door. Tweedledum called over his shoulder, "Happy birthday, Bosh and Blurb!"

"Contrariwise!" shouted Tweedledee.

ON HUMANITY AND HUMUS

(Latin *homo*, man, and *humus*, earth, are etymologically akin,
as in "human," "humble," "humiliate," "posthumous")

Her urgent dust admits the thrust
Of urgent dust wherefrom
In hurricane of blood and pain
New urgent dust must come.

Since man in dust is drawn, and shall
Resolve into the same,
We walk a road umbilical,
Attested by a name:

For homo, *man, and* humus, *earth,*
Though seeming two, are one,
Together facing from their birth
Annihilation.

As man and dust, so life and death
Are one, and Christ and clod—
Their common heritage the breath
Inspired, expired, of God.

(It is no coincidence that the name of Adam, the first man,
approximates "from the ground.")

2

EXPLETIVE
DELETED

To "bowdlerize" is to delete from a book expressions considered indelicate or offensive. The verb memorializes Dr. Thomas Bowdler, an amiable English gentleman who in the first quarter of the nineteenth century gave up his medical practice at sixty-four to perform intimate surgery on the literary works of Shakespeare, Gibbon, and God. The word "bowdlerize" is first used in General Perronet Thompson's *Letters of a Representative to His Constituents During the Session of 1836*. It is thus eligible for my list of expressions with assured birthyears,* and in fact just days after that birthday visit with Lewis Carroll I was making a note to that effect when I heard someone clear his throat.

Looking up, I saw standing across from me a small elderly gentleman dressed in a coat of plain brown cloth, with a waistcoat, and brown breeches that fitted into riding boots. He stepped over to shake my hand, walking with a marked limp, his countenance alight with a friendly smile.

"I am Dr. Bowdler," he said. "I am grateful to you for remembering me. After all, I am generally considered an insignificant little man, and have been dead since 1825."

"Everyone remembers you," I assured him. "Why, on the two-hundredth anniversary of your birth—July 11,

* See the preceding chapter.

1954—a band of Swansea students laid a floral wreath on your tomb in Oystermouth church. It was a wreath made up of fig leaves."

"What a gracious tribute!"

"Only recently I heard a story of how bowdlerism persists in Britain. Two barges collided on a rainy day, and the owners sued and countersued. The judge was Scottish. He was also hard of hearing. Since he could not follow the robust Cockney of one of the witnesses, a lawyer acted as interpreter. The Cockney was asked, 'And were you surprised when you observed that a collision had occurred?' The answer, as rendered by the lawyer, was 'I was completely taken aback.' "

"Is that all the story?"

"Of course. It was a bowdlerism after your own heart. What the witness had actually said was 'Cor, you could 'ave buggered me through me oilskins!' "

"I fear," he said gently, "that you misinterpret the cleansing work my sister and I sought to do. We did not hope to purge the language of the bargeman or the fish merchant. No, we dealt only with great literature, and then omitted only those words and expressions which cannot with propriety be read aloud in a family."

"I gather that your sister was a great help to you."

"Yes, bless her, she worked day and night."

"Blushes must often have colored her innocent cheek."

"Alas, yes; but she persevered. I could hardly tear her away from her research."

"She'd be still busier today, I imagine."

"Yes. She often says to me, 'Thomas, if only you and I could return to our labors! What a great work there is to be done!' And she is right. From what I hear, scarcely a novel of the day is not lewd, lascivious, or scatological —and generally all three."

"You are absolutely right," I said. "The sort of pornographic book that circulated underground in your time is out on coffee tables now. In fact, I happen to own one written by a man named Roger Bowdler, who says he is your great-great nephew."

He winced, and I felt ashamed of myself for upsetting him. But then his face brightened. "Would you mind," he said, "if I borrowed the book, and perhaps did a little red-inking?"

"By the time you finished," I said, "there would be nothing left."

"Nonetheless, Harriet and I would be grateful for the loan. You, sir, seem a respectable sort; could I not perhaps persuade you to take up the crusade against indelicacy where my sister and I had to drop it?"

"I'm one step ahead of you. I have a proposal in the works that will really clean up the English language."

"May I ask what it is, sir?"

"Well, not many people are aware that a lot of perfectly respectable words have impolite beginnings. We pass those ugly meanings back and forth in talking, without realizing it. I call those words whited sepulchers. They are polluting the language, and I propose to get rid of them."

"I am not sure I follow you," said Dr. Bowdler.

"Take, for instance, 'schism.' Surely, you would say, a respectable word?"

"Indeed—frequently applied to a separation or division in the Christian Church."

"Ah!" said I. "Yet 'schism' is etymologically associated with 'shit.' "

He paled.

"I give you likewise 'poppycock.' I give you 'coccagee,' the cider apple. I give you the lovely 'cowslip' and 'oxlip.' "

"You do not mean—"

"Indeed I do. All named after excrement. 'Poppy-

39

cock' hobson-jobsons Dutch *pappekak,* 'soft dung.' 'Coccagee' corrupts Irish *cac a' ghéidh,* 'dung of a goose,' after the greenish-yellow color shared by the goose dung and the apple."

"What do you mean by 'hobson-jobson'?"

"To substitute familiar English sounds for words borrowed from another language. Shiite Moslems have a custom of mourning for the two slain grandsons of Mahomet at the festival of Muharram by crying ritually, *'Ya Hasan, ya Husayn'*—'O Hasan, O Husain!' The English replaced Hasan and Husain with two good old English names, Hobson and Jobson. But 'cowslip' and 'oxlip' aren't hobson-jobsons. They are flowers found in pastures, and are called after the droppings of cattle."

"I disclaim such profane etymologies."

"Let me give you one that came into use after your time. In the 1840s a New York attorney named Scheuster became notorious for his pettifogging tactics, and the name, corrupted into 'shyster,' came to mean a tricky lawyer. Now, *Schuster* is simply German for 'shoemaker'; but *Scheuster* became 'shyster' because of the sound association with *Scheisse*—German for, again, 'shit.' "

"I see no problem in 'shyster.' It is vulgar slang, easily dropped."

"Do you remember the word 'petar,' or 'petard,' in *Hamlet?* Shakespeare said, 'For 'tis the sport to have the enginer/Hoist with his own petar.' A petar was a sort of overgrown firecracker, used in war to make a breach in a wall. It was set off by a fuse, and if the fuse burned too fast the man who lighted it might be blown up in the explosion."

"I remember the word. What is wrong with it?"

"It must go. It derives from Latin *pedare,* 'to fart.' "

"If only I had known!"

" 'Partridge' has to go for the same reason. The bird

makes a sharp whirring sound when flushed—like the breaking of wind—so the Greeks called it *perdix*, 'the farter.' "

"But the first Perdix," objected Dr. Bowdler, "was the nephew and apprentice of Daedalus, the Greek artificer who shaped wings for himself to escape from the tyrant Minos. Perdix invented the saw and made the first pair of compasses. When Daedalus out of envy tried to kill Perdix by pushing him off a high tower, Minerva changed him into a partridge to save his life. There is no connection with breaking wind."

"A strong tail wind would have helped," I said. "Besides, she may have noticed that the poor fellow was a victim of flatulence."

"Just between us two, no ladies being present," said Bowdler, lowering his voice and winking, man-to-man, "there is an anecdote involving partridges that, though it has no scatological overtones, does have bawdy implications. When King Louis XV was reproached by his confessor for changing mistresses so frequently, he asked the priest to name his favorite food. '*Perdix*, your Majesty,' was the answer. 'From now on,' said Louis, 'you shall have *perdix* at every meal.' Months later the King asked the confessor how he was faring. 'Alas!' mourned the priest, raising his eyes to heaven; '*perdix, perdix, toujours perdix!*' . . . 'Ah, now you understand,' said the King."

Since Bowdler apparently considered that a pretty racy story, I laughed as if I had never heard it before. Then I went on:

"I'm going to get rid of the word 'breeches,' too. They cover a man's private parts, which makes them unspeakable. My book will substitute asterisks for 'breeches,' except in this one couplet:

> Though the region itches,
> Do not scratch your breeches.

" 'Bracket' is just as bad. It has the same etymological origin as 'breeches,' and in both architecture and typography a bracket looks considerably like a codpiece."

"Is it possible," said Dr. Bowdler, hesitantly, "that your proposals might be a trifle extreme? I am entirely on your side, of course; but had I still been alive in the time of the Victorians, I could never have agreed with their insistence on eliminating unfortunate word associations by calling a cock a rooster, an ass a donkey, or the leg of a chair a limb. That kind of euphemizing turned modesty into absurdity, and I am glad it has fizzled out."

"Aha!" I exclaimed. " 'Fizzle'! From the obsolete verb *fist*—again meaning to break wind, but silently."

"Are you making sport of me?"

"Not at all. Keep countenance, Dr. Bowdler. But remember that 'keep countenance' is the etymological equivalent of 'keep continent'—that is, hold your bowels and bladder under control."

"I have only your testimony on that," said Dr. Bowdler.

" 'Testimony'!" I cried triumphantly. "A perfect example of my point! It is from Latin *testis*, meaning both 'testicles' and 'witness.' When a man testified in court, he placed his hand over his most precious part—his testicles, the container of his seed. His testicles were witness to his virility, as his testimony was witness to his credibility. Down with 'testimony'—'testify'—'testament'! Out with them all!"

"Out with them all," agreed Dr. Bowdler, sounding uncertain.

"Have you ever eaten an avocado? Or admired an orchid?"

He nodded.

"The Nahuatl Indians named the avocado, because of its shape, *ahuacatl*, meaning testicle. The Greeks named the orchid, for the same reason, from their word for the same organ. And how about 'coquette'?"

He shook his head.

"It is a miniaturized and feminized version of 'cock,' for penis. 'Porcelain'?"

"I am not sure I want to know."

" 'Porcelain' is from Latin *porcella,* 'little sow.' The earthenware looks like the cowrie shell, which is supposed to look like a sow's vulva."

Dr. Bowdler was beginning to glance longingly at the door. I continued:

" 'Footling' means 'foolish, trifling.' But where does it come from?"

He shook his head again.

"From French *foutre*—'to copulate with.' By the way —have you ever eaten matzo balls?"

"I am afraid I don't know what they are."

"They are balls of seasoned, unleavened flour, used in soup. 'Matzo' comes from Hebrew-Arabic *massah,* 'to touch, handle, squeeze, as unleavened bread.' The word is indecent."

"But why?"

"Because 'massage' has the same root. And 'massage parlor' comes from 'massage.' You certainly don't approve of massage parlors, do you?"

"Oh, dear, I should rather not hear about them."

"Then tell me this, Dr. Bowdler—do you agree that the word 'paramour' should be dropped from respectable literature?"

"Of course. A paramour is a lover or mistress, generally illicit. It is from French *par,* 'by,' plus *amour,* 'sexual love.' "

"But 'paramour' has a reverse twist. Its origin could scarcely be more holy. The early Christians used it to describe the relationship between God and the Virgin Mary."

He shook his head despondently.

"Or take 'madrigal,'" I continued relentlessly. "A lovely word, you say, for a lovely song, praising the Virgin. Yet what the madrigal actually celebrates is the *matrix*, Greek for 'womb,' in this case Mary's womb, because it was there that Christ took physical shape. I know you would not want the word 'womb' to be mentioned before an innocent child."

This time he did not agree. "To me, sir," said Dr. Bowdler, "the womb whence God emerged partakes of God's own purity."

"All right. Then how about 'hey nonny nonny,' the traditional refrain in old verses?"

"How can you object to that? Nobody would cut from *As You Like It* the stanzas beginning:"

> It was a lover and his lass,
> With a hey, and a ho, and a hey nonino . . .

"I would. And I will. 'Hey-nonny-no' was a camouflage for indelicate allusions—what Michael Drayton called 'these noninos of filthie ribauldry.' I would also toss 'intercourse' out of the language; we have come to use it only for sexual intercourse. The word 'occupy' has to go; indeed, it did vanish from proper company in the seventeenth and eighteenth centuries because it had been commonly used in the sense of 'to have to do with sexually.' And 'conversation': it was once all but taboo because 'criminal conversation' meant illegal cohabitation. Out! During the Vietnam War, President Johnson visited Australia to make a speech in which he had planned to say, 'Our soldiers who have passed through wish to be remembered to you.' An aide pointed out barely in time that 'to pass through' in Australia meant 'to copulate.' Oh, the tightrope our language must walk to preserve its purity is a narrow one

—narrower even than you, Dr. Bowdler, may have realized. Why, among the common meanings of 'enjoy'
was once 'to enjoy by possessing, as the rejoicing between a man and a woman.' I shall hate to see that word
go—it is beautiful—yet go it must."

Dr. Bowdler got to his feet. "I shall have to discuss
these matters with my sister," he said. "Forgive me, sir,
if I say that I suspect you have been speaking in part
with tongue in cheek."

Then his face lit up in the radiant smile it had worn
when I first saw him, and he said (I shall always love
him for it), "Good night, my friend. You will forgive me
if I fizzle off now."

"The next time," I said as he turned away with most
of my salacious books under his arm, "I will hold my
tongue and let you do the talking. Keep countenance,
Dr. Bowdler."

WORDS TOO, HIPPOCRATES

Words too, Hippocrates, in flesh are sown;
    From human entrails verbal offspring burst;
1. *"Jade" is the offspring of a* colic stone;
2.   *"Pygmy" and "Pugilist" were* fist *at first;*
3. *And "Algebra," "the setting of a bone."*
4.   *A "Bellows" apes the panting* belly's *thirst;*
5. *"Hysteria" is loosened* womb *a-groan;*
6.   *"Exuberance" at* udder's *teat was nursed.*

7. *Should you in dream meet mighty Mastodon,*
    Bow down; his name reveres your mother's breast—
So nipple-like the tubercles upon
    Those teeth wherewith his hay is ground and pressed.
8. *(And Hypochondria finds worried home in*
    A niche beneath the ribs of your abdomen.)

1. Jade, a hard mineral (from Spanish *piedra de ijada,* colic stone). 2. Pygmy, Pugilist (from Greek *pugme,* fist; the pugilist because he fights with his fists, and the Pygmy because he is fist-size). 3. Algebra (from Arabic *al + jebr,* reunion of broken parts). 4. Bellows (from Old English *bel(i)g,* belly). 5. Hysteria (from Greek *hystera,* womb). 6. Exuberance, a condition of unrestrained high spirits (from Latin *uber,* fertile, related to "udder"). 7. Mastodon (from Greek *mastos,* breast, + *odont,* tooth). 8. Hypochondria (Greek "region under the ribs," once held to be the seat of melancholy).

3

THE VOYAGE OF
THE GURGLE

LANGUAGE may be too good for the likes of us. Certainly Caliban held that opinion when he complained to Prospero in *The Tempest:*

> You taught me language; and my profit on't
> Is, I know how to curse! The red plague rid you,
> For learning me your language!

And if we do not deserve language, surely we do not deserve writing. The Egyptian god Ammon scolded his associate Thoth for teaching writing to mankind:

> This discovery of yours will create forgetfulness in the learners' souls, because they will not use their memories; they will trust to the external written characters and not remember themselves. The specific which you have discovered is an aid not to memory, but to reminiscence, and you give your disciples not truth, but only the semblance of truth; they will be hearers of many things and will have learned nothing; they will appear to be omniscient, and will generally know nothing; they will be tiresome company, having the show of wisdom without its reality.

All very well—but where did those sounds and letters and words and sentences that make up verbal communication come from, anyway?

Charles Darwin, a hundred years dead, came visiting. He was gloomy of countenance, and at first glance seemed a forbidding figure. A black cape enveloped him; his white brows beetled; his beard sprang out from the sides of his face and billowed down his front like an untrimmed hedge; his top was bald. The reason he gave for the visit surprised me: he was hoping I might be willing to play backgammon with him for an hour or so.

"My health was bad for most of my later years," he said, "which saved me from the distractions of society and amusement. I also had no need to earn my own bread, which, combined with my ill health, left me ample leisure to carry on my studies. My only diversion, save for a daily walk, was to play backgammon of an evening with my dear wife, Emma. Now I no longer have work to pursue, and I find myself restless; I was glad to learn there was someone living on whom I might pay a social call."

So we played, and he trounced me twice running. I suspected, though, that there was another reason for his visit, and I was right. When I proposed a third game in order to redeem myself, he shook his head.

"The fact is," he said, "that I have another reason for being here. I have a problem; and I am told that you might be able to help."

"I certainly will if I can. What is the problem?"

"Perhaps you know that I once wrote a book called *The Voyage of the Beagle,* describing an expedition during which I studied the development of animal species. As it happens, one of the amenities of my present residence is a well-stocked library, and the other evening it occurred to me to reread that book for the first time in a hundred and fifty years."

"And?"

"Sir, someone had rewritten my book. It was a pirated edition—scandalously abused."

"In what way?"

"In the first place, the title has been changed to *The Voyage of the Gurgle.* See for yourself—I have brought the book with me. Why, the very first sentence is all wrong. My observations took place in and around South America, but the sentence reads:

> After having been twice driven back by heavy southwesterly gales, Her Majesty's ship *Gurgle,* a sesquipedalian brig, under the command of Captain Fitz Roy, R.N., sailed from Davenport on the 27th of December, 1831, and on the 10th of October, 1832, reached the recently discovered island of Vocalia, in the South Pacific Ocean five hundred miles east of New Zealand.

"It was common for ships to be blown off course in those days," I said.

"No—the destination was deliberate. Listen:

> It was my particular commission to study the animal life, which proved so unprecedented, filling the air of Vocalia with such an extraordinary battery of sounds, that one must wonder if the native fauna may be in truth proto-animals—mere vocalizations which through a caprice of nature have taken on the semblance of life.

"The reason I have resorted to you," he said, "is this: I have been told that you have an interest, amateurish but intense, in the branch of knowledge generally lumped under the name of language. You may be in a position to discover and expose the fiend who pirated my book. And that is not all. Perhaps"—he looked at me out of haunted eyes—"this *is* the book I wrote, after

53

all. Perhaps the book is right, and my memory is wrong. Then a further question arises. If I really did visit the island of Vocalia, did I encounter breathing creatures there, or animated letters of the alphabet? You may be able to help me find out."

"I cannot comment without knowing a lot more."

"Then listen to these paragraphs:"

The inhabitants are a tribe consisting now of fewer than a hundred Bushmen, who have no recollection of how or when their forebears reached the island. The fauna is extremely limited in variety, but overwhelming in numbers. I could not take a walk without stepping on living things, bumping into them, or having them alight on me. Their outcries are intense and senseless. To sleep, I had to shut off my hearing with a pillow.

Birds are the most advanced of the fauna, but slugs and insects are by far the most common. These fill the air and the earth with screeching, howling, and humming. The slugs sound like Billingsgate fishwives with cleft palates. The birds scream, moan, rage. From the totality of sources there emerge claps as of thunder, clackety-clacks as of water mills, rattlings as of iron wheels bouncing over cobble stones; gasps; sighs; hoots of laughter.

The insects have shapes like the letters of the alphabet. Because of their appearance and the special sounds characteristic of each variety, I have called the flying sort, which drift about on varicolored, butterfly-like wings, *Vowels;* and the wingless ones, which hitch along like worms or walk about on many-jointed, spindly legs, looking like the stick-figures drawn by children, *Consonants.* They do not stridulate, but utter sounds from their mouths. They often combine in links, which occasionally form coherent words, or even sentences; I once found a string of insects, in the lee of a stone, so arranged as to spell out the prediction "We think it will rain"; I assume the effect was a matter of chance, yet each individual in the string was holding a tiny red umbrella over its head.

"I am beginning to suspect," I said, "that you have been trapped, or think you have, in some warp of metaphor, and I assume you fear the metaphor may be leading your scientific observations astray. Yet it is perfectly possible that you were simply the first naturalist to come across a new manifestation of life, as the first visitors to Australia discovered kangaroos. Still more exciting, the entire notion of an alphabet may have originated on this island of yours, and spread thence to the rest of the world. Rather than worrying, then, why not take pride in being a semantic pioneer?"

"I hope you will draw no conclusions until you know more of what I found there," he said. "If the account in *Gurgle* is correct, for instance, there are major distinctions between the Consonants and their natural prey, the Vowels. The Consonants have no natural enemies save for a creature remotely of their own kind, a monstrously overgrown Bee."

" 'Bee' is certainly a consonant."

"I am not in a mood for levity. The Consonants pass their lives on the ground or in trees. The Vowels, on the other hand, are creatures of water and air. They settle on the surfaces of ponds to lay their eggs, which float about in spherical little cases until the larvae hatch, by the millions. These, after spending several months skating about like water bugs, sprout gauzy wings and fly off to their fate, which is to be eaten; in the daytime birds pick them off in midair, while at night, when the Vowels settle to earth to sleep, they fall prey to the slugs and Consonants. The Bushmen contend that the reason

the creatures of Vocalia utter only inarticulate sounds is
that they eat only vowels."

"Physiologists agree," I said, "that animals lack vocal
organs capable of forming consonants. In verse it would
go something like this:"

THERE'S NO B IN BARK, BABY

I thought I heard a terrier
  A-barking gaily at a cat.
No sound, said I, is merrier
  Than that.

Pooh-pooh, said you, the *b* and *k*
  Are but phantasms of your head;
Dogs can't articulate that way,
  You said.

With dripping udder lowed a cow;
  I thought she mooed to call her calf—
The gentlest sound of all, I vow,
  By half.

Pooh-pooh, said you, a cow can't moo;
  For want of suck, the cow is *ooh*-ing.
The *m* of moo is all in you—
  Your doing.

Some irate ducks went quacking off,
  Their sound one loud Achillean cuss.
No noise, said I, is more cacoph-
  Onous.

Pooh-pooh, said you, you only fanc-
  Y that the sound you hear is quacking;
The skills ducks need for consonants
  Are lacking.

I thought I heard a stallion neigh,
    And neighing back, I thought, a mare.
I said, there's horsing on the way,
    I swear.

Pooh-pooh, said you; as Rover ut-
    Ters "Ah," Duck "A," Cow "Oo,"
So horse says "Eigh"; the *n* is but
    In you.

Yet still I hear (though by ill luck
    The consonants indeed be lacking)
Dog bark, Cow moo, Horse neigh, and Duck
    A-quacking.

Mr. Darwin forced a smile.

"To summarize, then," I said, "Vocalia is overrun with primitive creatures having the appearance of letters of the alphabet and making a broad spectrum of inarticulate sounds. Am I right so far?"

"Yes, if I really made the voyage. But the situation is more complex than that. Here is another passage from *Gurgle:*"

Among the fauna is a land slug, the Aei. It is beautifully colored with longitudinal stripes, and consists of many sub-orders, indistinguishable in appearance, yet never interbreeding. Each of these sub-orders makes only one sound, and eats only the Vowel or Vowels representing that sound in appearance. For instance, a given Aei may confine its diet to the sound of soft *e,* as in b*e*d or r*e*d. But the victim does not have to be the *shape* of an *e;* it can be shaped like *ai* as in s*ai*d, or *a* as in *a*ny; the sound, not the appearance, is what counts. An Aei that lives on the sound of short *i* will readily accept as food the *y* of ab*y*ss, the *u* of b*u*sy, the *o* of w*o*men, the *e* of pr*e*tty, the *ie* of s*ie*ve, or the *ui* of g*ui*lt.

"Clearly," I said, "Vocalian slugs make the same distinction in their eating that we do in our spelling. If an English word is pronounced with a given vowel sound —nei*gh*, for instance, with the sound of long *a*—the appropriate vowels in the word have to adapt themselves to that sound, whether they like it or not."

"Some Vocalian predators apply the same principle in exactly the opposite sense," said Darwin. "Listen:"

A Vocalian water bird called the Ouy has short legs, web feet, extremely long-pointed wings, and is about the size of a tern. In a lake from which the water had been nearly drained, and which in consequence was thick with the larvae of skating Vowels, I saw several of these birds flying rapidly backwards and forwards close to the surface. They kept their bills wide open, and the lower mandibles half buried in the water, dexterously managing thus to scoop up fleeing Vowels in huge numbers; yet later, when I had occasion to examine the contents of the crops of several slain Ouys, I found that each bird had managed unerringly to pick out the one particular Vowel on which it lived. And here it was its physical resemblance to that letter of the alphabet which counted. An Ouy that lived only on the vowel *o* would choose *o* with equal readiness whether it was pronounced as in g*o*ne, l*o*ne, *o*ne, or w*o*men.

I leaned forward in my chair. "The parallel to our English usage continues to be striking," I said. "Schoolboys have great fun with the fact that in b*ou*gh the *ou* sound is pronounced as in n*ow;* in f*ou*ght as in d*o*g; in r*ou*gh as in st*u*ff; in th*ou*gh as in n*o;* in thr*ou*gh as in g*oo*. As far as the printed page goes, there is no distinction between the vowel sounds of *ea*rth and h*ea*rt."

"Vowels," said Mr. Darwin, "have been compared to

the flesh of the body, and consonants to the skeleton which keeps it upright. Following this analogy, I would have thought that Vocalian birds, having a complete skeletal structure, would be able to articulate. But according to my report—if it *is* my report—this is not generally so. *Gurgle* says:"

The Aoi is a large flightless bird resembling the emu. It uses its wings as the brig *Gurgle* uses its canvas, to catch the wind. These birds run at great speed close-hauled; yet at the start they expand their wings, and like a vessel make all sail.

But the Aoi is, despite its elaborate skeletal structure, entirely mute, save in the one situation whence its name is derived.

Bushmen hunt it with a weapon consisting of two roundish stones in nets, united by a thin cord about eight feet long, plaited from a tough seaweed abundant off the coast. The Bushman whirls these stones round and round his head; then, taking aim, sends them like chain shot revolving through the air. They no sooner strike their victim than, winding round it, they cross each other, and become firmly hitched. At that instant, knowing its death to be imminent, the bird utters the dolorous cry "A-o-i"—the very word, you may recall, that closes so many stanzas of the medieval French epic *Chanson de Roland*. It epitomizes ultimate despair, as in the wailing of the French after their bloody loss at Roncesvalles in 778.

(I was briefly distracted, first trying to imagine how large flightless birds could have become involved in the battle of Roncesvalles, and then how the remnants of the flock could have made their way to an unknown island halfway around the world. When my attention flitted back to Mr. Darwin, he was still reading:)

I come now to two species of birds which, however the Bushmen may deny the evidence of their own ears, do clearly articulate. The Mama bird, dull brown, and the size of a starling, is difficult to observe because it prefers to remain secluded in the forest. I managed nonetheless to see one clearly through my glass, and can attest that its beak is lined with a lip-like tissue. Its call resembles the wailing of a child for its mother: "Ma-ma, ma-ma." A vibration first builds up inside the closed beak, which then opens suddenly; the *m* in the "ma" that emerges is unmistakable.

I conclude that I have been privileged to be the first naturalist actually to hear a consonant pronounced by a bird.

I interrupted here. "Most philologists believe," I said, "that *m* was also the first consonant to be pronounced by human beings. When our vocal apparatus had developed sufficiently, *m* must have emerged from the mouth of some paleolithic infant, to the astonishment of the mother:"

IN PRAISE OF M,
MOTHER OF CONSONANTS

The while its appetite was slack,
  The sated babe said "Ah!"
But hunger set its lips a-smack,
  And "Ah" came out as "Ma,"
For "breasts—the milk therein—a snack!"
  Hence *Mom,* for whom hurrah!

It was an inappropriate interjection, and I apologized. "The fact is," I said, "that though your story fascinates me, I can't see how I can possibly help."

"I am about to tell you; but first let me mention the

second species of bird on Vocalia which articulates. It is the green-necked Bopper. When a flock settles on the water, they at once burst into a plosive tumult, like the sounds one hears emerging from the doors of a saloon. The consonants they use are *b* and *p*."

"Formed, like *m*," I said, "by first closing the lips. Do they also pronounce *d* and *t?*"

"The book does not say so."

"Then they have a long way to go before they can develop language. *D* and *t*, which require setting the tongue against the roof of the mouth, supposedly followed *b* and *p* in human speech. The other consonants came later. *L* and *r* were last; they are so recent in our history that *l* does not yet exist among the Japanese, or *r* among the Chinese."

Mr. Darwin cleared his throat. "I have a more specific favor to ask of you than I may have indicated," he said.

"Anything I can do, of course."

"I must be frank; you would not have been my first choice for this mission. But it appears that you are the only living person on whom we of earlier generations are free to call if you invite us. Frankly, I do not understand the reason for this. . . ."

"No more do I."

"But in any event, there it is. I should be your eternal debtor, sir, if you would arrange an expedition to visit the area where the island of Vocalia may or may not exist. The longitude is 150 degrees west, the latitude 43 degrees south. If there is a Vocalia, I have no wish to be credited with its discovery; that honor will go to you. If there is not, I shall rest the better for knowing that I did not at one point in my lifetime suffer from a most horrid and peculiar hallucination."

I shook my head. "Not a chance," I said. "I haven't the money, and I haven't the time. Besides, there isn't an inch of the South Pacific that hasn't been mapped. If there ever was a Vocalia, it sank under the water long ago."

He nodded sadly. "Ah, well," he said, "I knew there was little hope. But would you at least do one thing for me? I'd like to leave my copy of *The Voyage of the Gurgle* with you. Dip into it from time to time. Just possibly it may lead you to change your mind."

"I doubt that," I said. "But I'll certainly read the book. Anyway, come back soon for another backgammon match."

"I'll be glad to," said Mr. Darwin. "But please don't feel obliged to invite me. Frankly, you aren't much of a backgammon player."

CASH
(French *caisse*, box)

The French say caisse *for "box."*
Since in one's box one locks
One's money, like a flash
We turned caisse *into* cash.
I'm sorry to confess
No cash *is in my* caisse.

4

BY DAY I AM AN EMPTY ROOM

A HANDSOME black German shepherd dog came visiting, drawing by a leash an aging man with an abbreviated white beard and dark glasses. The old man wore a dingy white robe and poked about with a white cane. He gave his name as Homer, and said he had come from ancient Greece to warn me about riddles. "I died of one," he said.

I led him to an easy chair by the fire, saw him settled with the German shepherd at his feet, and asked, "How so?"

"At vexation of not being able to find the answer."

"Do you recall the riddle?"

"How could I forget? It was 'What we caught we threw away, and what we could not catch we kept.' "

"Everyone knows the answer to that," I said.

"Impossible!"

"The answer, Homer, is 'fleas.' "

"Fleas!" he screamed. "And for this I had to die?"

Homer was too upset at having been so easily hoodwinked to stay more than a few minutes, but even so he managed to turn my mind to riddles, a subject that had not theretofore been among my pressing concerns. I went through the books of riddles on my shelves, read histories of them in my encyclopedias, and wound up by turning several of them into verse.

First, though, I had to decide just what I meant by a riddle. In one dictionary sense, it is a sieve with coarse meshes for sifting grades of potatoes or coal. In another, it is a board having a row of pins, set zigzag, between which wires are drawn to straighten them. Then again, it is a container holding thirteen bottles of wine. It is a verb meaning to separate, as grain from chaff, or perforate, as to riddle with bullets.

Most familiarly, though, a riddle is a question that contains a seeming paradox or contradiction, an enigma that invites a playful sort of guessing. It is this kind of riddle which killed Homer. Yet the other riddles are also germane; for though there is no etymological linkage, there is an analogy between the potato sifter, the row of pins, the verb meaning to separate, and the word game: all attempt to clarify matters.

The first riddles sprang from man's perception of analogies in nature. The famous riddle of the Sphinx put such an analogy in the form of a question: What creature walks in the morning upon four legs, at noon upon two, and at evening upon three? The answer, of course, is man—as a baby on hands and feet, as an adult erect on two legs, and in old age with a staff. Once the analogy between the stages of life and the notion of a creature with a changing number of limbs was observed, the riddle sprang into being full-blown.

Other sources of riddles are animism (the personification of nature) and fable:

• What flies forever and rests never?
Answer: The wind

• What is wingless and legless, yet flies fast and cannot be imprisoned?
Answer: The voice

As plowed land intruded ever deeper into the surrounding wilderness, riddles gradually turned their attention from artless and primitive subjects to puzzles nearer home:

• You eat something that you neither plant nor plow. It is the son of water, but if water touches it, it dies.
   Answer: Salt

• What can go up a chimney down but can't come down a chimney up?
   Answer: An umbrella

There are also trick riddles with humdrum answers, of the sort we recall from our childhood:

• Why does a miller wear a white hat?
   Answer: To keep his head warm

In the footsteps of the folk riddle came the conundrum, a pun in the form of a question:

• What has a head and four legs but cannot walk?
   Answer: A bed

• Why did the lobster turn red?
   Answer: Because it saw the salad dressing

At call, insights submerged under the tide of workaday concerns surge suddenly, startlingly, back to the surface. Emotional wellsprings flush away the accumulation of leafy litter.

Whether because the best poetry has a quality of revelation or because the poetic voice came easier in the old days, riddles have often taken melodic form, as in this English-Scottish ballad:

I gave my love a cherry that has no stone.
I gave my love a chicken that has no bone.
I told my love a story that has no end.
I gave my love a baby with no cry-en.

How can there be a cherry that has no stone?
How can there be a chicken that has no bone?
How can there be a story that has no end?
How can there be a baby with no cry-en?

A cherry when it's blooming has no stone.
A chicken when it's pipping has no bone.
The story that I love her has no end.
A baby when it's sleeping there's no cry-en.

That is scarcely great poetry; but it is charming. And
charm is its own reason for being.

After Homer's visit, I passed several tranquil evenings
at the house on Fifty-first Street turning prose riddles
into rhymes. The results follow. There is no consistency
about the structure of either riddles or rhymes: question and answer may both appear in the verse itself; the
answer may be appended; or both question and answer
may be implicit. Occasionally I have inserted blanks that
invite you to guess the solution.*

Let us begin with the heavens:

1. *from Russia*
   The old woman's starving mutt
   Spies above the hut
   A toothsome crust of bread.
   Ah, but

* The originals of the versified riddles appear at the end of the chapter.

It's way above his head;
He barks, unfed.

Answer: The crescent moon

2. *from Japan*
   The bald head called up to the moon,
   "We two are like as two old shoon."
   Pressed this likeness to define,
   He said, "We both are round, and shine."

3. *from Ceylon*
   By day I am an empty room;
   By night, a garden in full bloom.

   Answer: The sky

4. *from Persia*
   Ten thousand shining knights I call
       my own—
   Their lord am I.
   With golden banner rides one knight
       alone—
   Aghast, we fly.

   Answer: The stars, the moon, and the sun

These riddles bring heaven down to earth:

5. *from Japan (a haiku)*
   An autumn sky and
   Cloth poorly dyed—can you not
   See the resemblance?

   Answer: Both change color easily.

6. *from Europe*
   The way you said it
   Is not *comme il faut:*
   "What was made long ago,
   But I just made it?"

   > *Answer:* Either a bed, as claimed by the chamber-
   > maid, or the maid in the bed, as claimed by the
   > roomer.

7. *from Russia*
   If you have feared
      That maybe
   You might have a baby
      With a beard,
   Take note:
      Don't have a baby _____.

   > *Answer:* Goat

Our bodily parts are fair play for riddlers:

8. *from Ireland*
   The shortest short bridge in the
      world, I suppose,
   Is the bridge, is the bridge, is the bridge of my _____.

   > *Answer:* Nose

9. *from Europe*
   Why is it so
   That bald you grow
   With beard still black and curly?
   Your hair appeared
   Before your beard,
   And so departs more early.

Animal riddles are as common as frogs in a marsh—
and sometimes *are* frogs in a marsh:

10. *from Poland*
    A quick knight walks amid the bogs;
        His little friends all run away.
    Who is he, and who are they?

    Answer: He's a stork, and they are frogs.

11. *from Russia*
    "What kind of bush do you sit under,
    Rabbit, in the rain and thunder?"
    "The only kind that I can get—
    A bush that's _____."

    Answer: Wet

12. *from Ireland*
    The cow is broad, the cow is wide,
    But hairy only on one side.
    Which side? Just look at any cow;
    _____, I vow.

    Answer: Outside

13. *from India*
    They come from eggs . . .
        First get born . . .
    Then get legs.

    Answer: Frogs

14. *from Haiti*
    Answer, I implore,
        This enigma, love:

73

Four feet on the floor,
  Four feet above.

  Answer: A cat on a table

15. *from Tennessee*
  What is it that
  Has ears like a cat
  And a head like a cat
  And feet like a cat
  And a tail like a cat
  But for all that
  Is not a cat?

  Answer: A kitten

16. *from the Midwest*
  Answer me!
  What was not,
  What is not,
  What will never be?
  What? Haven't guessed?
  It's perfectly clear:
  A mouse's nest
  In a cat's ear.

17. *from Tibet*
  What babe, I beg,
    Is bald of crown
    And white as down
  When born? . . . _____.

  Answer: An egg

Riddles have a high old time with artifacts:

18. *from the Votiak tribe of Africa*
  Who judges truly,

Never fails,
Though he is lifeless?
Tell me! . . . _____.

   Answer: Scales

19. *from Iceland*
   Turn us on our backs, and then
   Open up our stomachs.
   You will wisest be of men,
   Though at start a lummox.

   Answer: Books

20. *from Persia*
   A silver serpent swam within an urn;
   A golden bird did in its mouth abide.
   The serpent drank the water; this in turn
   Dissolved the serpent; then the gold bird died.

   Answer: An oil lamp. (The serpent is the wick, the
   water is the oil, and the golden bird is the flame.)

21. *from the Kxatla tribe of Africa*
   "Mother, say
      When I dance
   Why you stay
      Still, askance?"
   "So't must be.
      Child is branch—
   Mother, tree."

The deepest riddles of all are hidden in our hearts.

22. *from ancient Greece*
   Though iron's strong, the Blacksmith, stronger still,
   Can beat and twist it.

What's then so strong that all the Blacksmith's will
Cannot resist it?

Answer: Love

23. *from Moslem lands*
Who holds me tight
Through the night
But at dawn's crack
Turns her back?

Answer: Sleep

24. *from Africa*
Bury deep;
    Heap on stones.
Yet will I
    Dig up the bones.

Answer: Memory

This final riddle offers hope that no tragedy is utter:

25. *from Jamaica*
In all the world, one ax;
    One man; one tree.
Man attacks
Tree with ax;
Tree, in fall
    (Ah me! ah me!),
Kills man, ax, all.
Who'll now recall
    That trinity—
Man, ax, tree?

Answer: The women

The original prose riddles are:

1. Over the old woman's hut hangs a crust of bread; the dog barks but cannot reach it. What is it?

2. How does the moon resemble a bald head?

3. In the morning the basket is empty. At night—a basket full of flowers.

4. Who is the king that travels with thousands of shining knights—yet when another knight appears alone with a yellow banner, the king and all his followers flee?

5. What is the resemblance between an autumn sky and poorly dyed cloth?

6. What is it was made years ago, but I just made it?

7. What baby is born with a beard?

8. What is the shortest bridge in the world?

9. Why does the hair grow gray before the beard?

10. A quick knight walks along the stream, and when the little friends see him they all run away. Who is he, and who are they?

11. What kind of bush does a rabbit sit under when it rains?

12. On what side of the cow is the most hair?

13. What creature is born first and gets its legs later?

14. What has four feet on the floor and four feet above?

15. What is it has ears like a cat, a head like a cat, feet like a cat, a tail like a cat, but isn't a cat?

16. Tell me something that never, never was and never shall be.

17. What is white-headed when it is born?

18. What can judge truly, though lifeless?

19. If you want to be wise, turn me over on my back and open up my belly. What am I?

20. I saw a silvery snake with a golden bird in its mouth, lying in a round cistern. The snake was drinking the water and the water was eating the snake. When the snake drank up all the water, the golden bird died.

21. Tell me why the children are dancing but their mother does not dance.

22. Which is stronger, love or iron? Answer: Love. Iron is strong, but the blacksmith can bend it; love can overcome the blacksmith.

23. What is it we always want and forget when it comes to us?

24. Checking my sources, I found no riddle answered by "memory." I did find "That which digs about in a deserted village," to which the answer was "The human heart, which turns to think of the past." Apparently "heart" changed to "memory" in my mind while I was writing the couplet.

25. Supposing there was only one tree left in the world, and one man, and one ax! The man cut down the tree with the ax, but the one tree fell and killed the one man. Who would be left to tell the tale?

This Jamaican riddle is reminiscent of a saying popular in my childhood, which went something like this:

> If all the men were one man,
> What a great man that would be!
> If all the axes were one ax,
> What a great ax that would be!
> If all the trees were one tree,
> What a great tree that would be!
> If all the seas were one sea,
> What a great sea that would be!
> And if that great man
> Took that great ax
> And chopped down that great tree
> And it fell into that great sea,
> What a great splash that would be!

CALIBER
(Arabic *qalib,* mold)

A caliber *(at first "a mold*
For making bullets") spread its span
To "bullet of the size so told,"
And thence to "quality of man."

5

THE VOYAGE OF THE GURGLE: TWO EXCERPTS

As I had promised Charles Darwin, I read *The Voyage of the Gurgle* attentively. At one point I even thought of trying to have it reissued, since the copy lent me by Mr. Darwin, and for which he may return any day, is certainly the only one extant. But his style is a bit antiquated for present-day readers; and besides, there is the matter of copyright. There is a touch of the presumptuous, it seems to me, in copyrighting a book written by someone else, especially when that someone is available to play an occasional game of backgammon with you, but is not in a position to enter a suit against you in court.

So I have compromised by selecting the two following excerpts for inclusion here.

ANOKE, A NOKE, AN OAK

Certain life forms in Vocalia have a capacity, limited elsewhere to lizards and the like, of shedding old members or growing new ones. The process appears to antedate similar changes in the development of English words.*

* About the fifteenth century, the article *a* or *an* in English was commonly written in combination with the substantive following it, as *anoke, anele, anest*. When article and substantive were separated, it took a while for a consensus to be reached between "a noke" and "an oak," "a neel" and "an eel," "a nest" and "an est."

I found, for instance, a family of sea-slugs, about five inches long, of a dirty yellowish color, spotted with purple. According to the Bushmen, at one time the males of this species had a long tail, subdivided into several wavering filaments. A single slug, seen dimly through the delicate sea-weeds of its habitat, might be mistaken for a whole school of the crawlers.

This apparent multiplicity frightened off females who, preferring romance on an individual and private basis, were reluctant when a lover seemed not one but many. In order to perpetuate the species, the male slugs learned to retract their tails within their bodies. The retraction was reflected in their names; the slug known as the *Riddles,* for instance, shortened to the *Riddle,* and the *Skates* to the *Skate.*

In English too we shrank "riddles" to "riddle" and "skates" to "skate." We shortened the name *sherris,* a fortified wine from Jérez, Spain, to "sherry," and made the plural "sherries." When we adopted *cérise* and *chaise,* both singular, from the French, we made the singular forms in English "cherry" and "shay," the plural "cherries" and "shays."

The process was a practical one, for both the slugs and the language. Yet I like to imagine that when these Vocalian slugs foregather for vesper service, and send bubbling upwards through the water a music with the charm of an untuned hand organ, their retracted tails emerge once more, and one peering down through the drowned weeds would see them in their ancient form —not a truncated Riddle or Skate, but a full-blown Riddles or Skates.

There were other fauna too that paralleled words in their development, among them the following:

• The poisonous serpent formerly called *a Nadder* is now, by reason of the speed and accuracy with which it computes, called *an Adder.*

• The lizard once called *an Ewt* has swollen gigantically, besides developing suckers on its hinder feet; its name has increased with its size; it is today *a Newt*.

• The *Napron*—a toadlike monstrosity whose thick, dirt-resistant skin is often tanned by the Bushmen and used to protect the forward, subhemispheric parts of women—became *an Apron*.

• A bird the size of a raven, but of a dull green color save for a white flash on its belly, was once known as *an Eke*. Notable for its wide, horny feet, it nests in the most exposed situations, as on the top of a post, or, frequently, in a cactus. When pricked in its under parts by cactus needles, it cries, "Eek, eek," and was so named; but from the similarity of sound between *"an eke"* and *"a neke"* it was later called *neke,* and then, by a natural shift, *nick;* if asked to explain this transition, the Bushmen reply, "That is its *nick*name."

• The preferred food of the Nick is the Ouch. The front wings of this beetle are modified to form hard, jewel-radiant coverings which overlie the membranous rear wings when at rest. Because of its brilliant colors, the beetle was first named *Nouche,* or *Nouch,* from Late Latin *nusca,* "brooch." But by the time of the appearance of the King James Bible, *Nouch* had become *Ouch;* "And they wrought onyx stones," says Exodus 39:6, "inclosed in *ouches* of gold."

The Nick kills Ouches by stamping them with its horny feet; the aptness of the iridescent beetle's name cannot be lost on anyone who has ever heard it, as it splatters, utter the expiring interjection "Ouch!"

There is also a crab which lives on the coconut trees and grows to an enormous size. It would at first be thought quite impossible for any crab to open the strong husk of the coconut. The front pair of legs of this crustacean, however, terminate in very heavy pincers shaped like a corkscrew. With these the crab bores through the husk, fiber by fiber, till an opening is made. Then, turning its body around, by the aid of its posterior and narrow pair of pincers it extracts and eats the white albuminous substance. The crab was originally called *a Nauger,* but again the first letter dropped away, and it is now styled *an Auger,* a name which has been borrowed in the English language for a type of drill.

Finally, there swims off the Vocalian shore a fish little more than four inches from snout to tail which has the singular power of distending itself into a nearly spherical form. So enhanced, it will push its way with insouciance into schools of much larger fish and herd them about at will, as a teacher might order the activities of children in a school-yard. The fish was known first as *a Noumpire,* then *a Numpire,* and finally *an Umpire.*

All these evolutions have their counterparts in the English language.

THE SPELLING BEE

. . . Curiously, the Bushmen of Vocalia are preoccupied with spelling. I say curiously since they do not communicate by writing, and so have no need to spell at all. They do not even know the meaning of the words they spell. Their fascination with the discipline derives from being surrounded by living letters, which they see taking shape repeatedly in words and strings of words.

As hunting skills determine status among aborigines elsewhere, so do spelling skills among the Bushmen of Vocalia. The chieftainship of the tribe is rotated every four weeks, going to the winner of a spelling contest held at the time of the full moon.

At moonrise on the evening of the contest, the tribefolk carry into a meadow outside their village woven sacks containing hundreds of Consonants, captured during the day, and Vowels, plucked from their sleeping places after sunset. The insects are emptied from the sacks into a pile, in which they remain, too drowsy to think of crawling away.

They are even too drowsy to respond to the attraction exerted over them by the mutated Spelling Bee which acts as judge of the contest. The Bee is a monstrous creature, nearly two feet high and twice as long. It was once a normal honey-bee, flitting from flower to flower, withdrawing sweet juices and fertilizing plants with pollen. But this particular Bee exuded a fragrance that drew nearby Vowels and Consonants as a moth is drawn to flame. The Bee discovered it preferred the taste of insects to that of blossoms, and gorged on them constantly. It grew so enormous that its wings, unable to bear it aloft, shrivelled away; it continued to swell until it could no longer drag itself about, but settled down permanently in the Bushmen's meadow. It had no need to move, for all insects within smelling-range of its fragrance come to it voluntarily, and compete to see which can most quickly scramble aboard the Bee's tongue, which it extends along the ground when hungry. When the tongue is crowded with insects, the Bee retracts it, swallows, and extends its tongue again for more.

The Bee has a mysterious gift: it knows the correct spelling of every word ever strung together by the insects of Vocalia. I have no idea how this remarkable faculty came to the attention of the Bushmen, but from time immemorial the Bee has been judging their spelling contests. Since the only sound it can emit is a buzz, a helper is required to call out the words to be spelled. This helper, known as the Announcer—as familiar with the pronunciation of words as is the Bee with their spelling—is a grasshopper, the only one of that species on Vocalia; and a good thing, too, since it is as overgrown for a grasshopper as the Spelling Bee is for a bee.

The contestants are ten Bushmen chosen by lot. They

stand in a row before the Spelling Bee and the Announcer, with the heap of insects midway between. The rest of the tribe—men, women, children, and infants—watch intently in the background.

The Announcer calls out a word, in the opening stages an easy one. The first contestant steps forward, selects from the heap of insects those that he believes make up that word, and arranges them in order on the Spelling Bee's tongue. If his spelling is right, the Bee swallows the insects; if not, it spits them out, buzzing irately, and the player is eliminated. As the game goes on, the words grow more difficult to spell. When only one contestant remains—generally at about the time the moon is at its zenith—he is proclaimed the chief of the tribe until the next full moon, and the Vocalians drift homewards after reverently singing the song translated here:

WHY SOUND MUST RUN,
AND SPELLING LAG BEHIND

The Bee its spelling carefully arranged,
But looked around, and found the Sound had changed;
For Etymology stuffs such a trove
Down Spelling's throat, the creature scarce can move,
While Sound's a hopper of a speed so rare
That when you see him he's no longer there.

One bygone aeon, Spelling dared Pronun-
Ciation to a race, and might have won—
Pronunciation, as a handicap,
Reclining in mid-race to take a nap.
But when the Bee approached, Sound oped his eyes,
Resumed the race, and hopped off with the prize.

Orthography since then prefers to stop
At home, and let Pronunciation hop.

ATROCIOUS
(Latin *ater* black + *oc* eye)

How did the word "atrocious" so become
The ne plus ultra *of opprobrium—*
An epithet of savage wickedness?
Well, here is etymology's best guess.

The Romans called "black" ater. *Adding* oc
(Their word for "eye"), they wound up with atroc-:
"Black-eyed." Now, people ebonous of eye
Were said to meet the Devil on the sly.

Hence, if you bang your eye against a knob,
The Devil has you by your thingumbob.
"Black-eyed—atrocious." (Dear, your eyes are gray;
You'd never be atrocious anyway.)

6

A POP OF LOLLIES,
A BELLY OF BONES

Forgotten words are mighty hard to rhyme.

OLD words never die. Look hard enough and you will find them, hidden in a thorn forest, sleeping away the centuries as sweetly as so many Snow Whites. A prince's kiss may yet return some of them to the bustle of the world.

President Harry S. Truman was no fairy-tale prince, and kissing was the last thing on his mind when he called someone who had offended him a "snollygoster." Nonetheless, he managed to stir that insulting epithet from a slumber that had lasted for fifty years or more. First recorded in the 1860s, the word had fallen asleep so quickly that scholars termed it nonce, meaning that it had sprung up to meet a passing need and then vanished.* The President told newsmen that a snollygoster was a man born out of wedlock. Students of word origins demurred; they said it meant a shyster lawyer. But the dispute is academic, since "bastard" and "shyster" are interchangeable in the vulgate. Whatever its correct meaning, "snollygoster" shows no sign of renewed drowsiness.

I suspect that the dictionary makers were slow to take on "snollygoster" in the first place. It is probably a natural child of Jacksonian Democracy, along with such

* I refer you to *Another Almanac of Words at Play* for Senator Charles McC. Mathias, Jr.'s, differing opinion on the spelling and etymology of the creature's name.

feisty siblings as "obsquatulate" (depart stealthily), "obflisticate" (obliterate), and "ramsquaddle" (beat up). None of these is around nowadays—but not because, like "snollygoster," they were born on the wrong side of the blanket. So were others that thrived nonetheless: "bodacious," "rip-roaring," "ripsnorter," "hornswoggle," "shebang," "shindig," "skedaddle," "splendiferous," "spondulicks," "slumgullion."

Even if I could, I would not kiss all obsolete English words back into the world; indeed, I would carefully avoid the bedchambers of several Snow Whites. I would go a long way around, for instance, to miss *"floccinauci-nihilipilification,"* said to be a linkage of words drawn from a sixteenth-century grammar of Latin. Eternal sleep is too good for such a jumble; surely it was used only in schoolboy jest.

But I would gladly give mouth-to-mouth resuscitation to "chantpleure." It is a chiaroscuric doublet from the French, and means "sing and weep at the same time." A lovely, lump-in-the-throat word.

"Acersecomic" is a forgotten expression that should have started from sleep spontaneously at the advent of the Beatles in the 1960s. It means "one whose hair is never cut," and is less pertinent today than it would have been a few years ago. But if there is a sleeping word meaning "one whose beard is untrimmed," it should wake up. We need it.

These reflections occurred to me as I sat in the library on Fifty-first Street rereading Susan Kelz Sperling's de-lightful *Poplollies and Bellibones.** As Curator of Forgot-ten Usage, she has catalogued some four hundred once familiar but now unremembered expressions. In fact, she has arranged them as if her book were a museum of natural history, in a succession of dioramas, each word

* Clarkson N. Potter, 1977.

posed like a stuffed animal in a replica of its habitat, looking as if alive. She used playlets, verses, and dialogues to place her poplollies in context.

"Poplolly," incidentally, was once a playful variant of "sweetheart," with slightly bawdy overtones. At first glance, "bellibone" is less winsome; it appears anatomical, even lewd. In fact it is a marvelous example of demotic wordplay. It is a hobson-jobson from French *belle et bonne* ("beautiful and good"), and means "dear and lovely maiden." The word fell out of favor several hundred years ago, perhaps because bellibones had become an endangered species. I am of two minds as to whether any survive today.

To identify words that have avoided obsoleteness by taking on new meanings, check any dictionary of the nineteenth century. In the 1896 *Encyclopaedic Dictionary,* for instance, you will find that a Martini is not a beverage mingling a dollop of gin with a drop of dry vermouth, as you think. Nor is it named for the Martini of Martini & Rossi, a firm that has long been famous for its reinforced wines. No; a Martini is

> The infantry fire-arm with which the English army has been armed since 1872. It is a combined weapon, the barrel being rifled on Henry's polygroove system, and the breech action being that invented by Martini. The action of opening the breech discharges the empty cartridge, which is partly formed of thin sheet brass, with a solid base-cup containing the detonating material, which also tends to prevent the escape of the powder-gas. It has a very flat projectory, a range of 1,200 yards for aimed fire, can discharge 25 unaimed shots per minute, has good penetration owing to its long bullet being slightly hardened by antimony, and rarely gets out of order.

In a number of respects this definition is applicable to the drink as well as the rifle. It would not surprise me if the same Martini invented both.

Most obsolete words will no doubt sleep on forever. Never again will we hear a crane crinkle, a sheep blore, or a donkey winx. Never again will we see a shiterow flap along a stream, though herons may abound. Nor shall I ever, provocation notwithstanding, dare call a son-in-law an odam, as the ancients did, accenting the last syllable.

A few of Susan Sperling's forgotten words are included in the *chant royal* below. I should like to think they will sense that their names have been spoken, and stir a moment in their sleep.

CHANTPLEURE

Said I to me, "A *chant royal* I'll dite;
Make much ado of words long laid away;
Cause eldnyng in the hearts of bards who cite
The sloomy phrases of Min Cheevy's day.
I'll chantpleure in the compass of a page;
Illumine man from show'ry spring till snow
In song all merry-sorry, con and pro."
I would have pulled it off, too, given time,
Had not a hidden ha-ha stubbed my toe:
Forgotten words are mighty hard to rhyme.

Ah, hadavist, in younghede, when from night
There dawned abluscent a fair morn in May
(The word for dawning, "sparrowfart," won't quite
Fit in here)—hadavist, I say,
That I'd in chair day by stoopgallant age
Be shabbed, adushed, pitchkettled, suggilled so,
Would I have been more hoful? Yes . . . or no.
One scantling bit of outwit's all that I'm
Quite sure of, after years of catch-and-throw:
Forgotten words are mighty hard to rhyme.

In younghede, ne'er a thrip gave I for blight
Of cark or ribble. I was ycore, gay;
Boonfellows matched me hum for hum, each wight
Aimcrying t'other, till as one we'd sway,
Turngiddy. Bashy beer could not assuage
Such thirst, nor kill-priest, even.
                    No Lothario
Outdid my eaubruche on Poplolly Row;
A fairhead who eyebit me in my prime
Soon knew my donge. (The meaning's clear, although
Forgotten words are mighty hard to rhyme.)

Pert draggle-tails first faged my appetite;
No inwit saved me from their shittle play.
Bedswerver, likewise housebreak, was I hight—
Poop-noddy at poop-noddy.
                    Now I pray
You fonkins may, like me, reach anchorage;
Find bellibone, as I did, to bestrow
The lip-clap seeds that into truehead grow—
So strown, we fellow-feel, and scrow-ward climb.
(Frush mubblefubbles. My own climb was slow:
Forgotten words are mighty hard to rhyme.)

Now on the wong at cockshut fades the light;
Birds' sleepy croodles cease. Not long to stay . . .
Once nesh as open-tide, I now affright . . .
Am lennow, spittle-ready . . . samdead clay,
A clutched bell-penny my remaining wage.
I wait, acclumsied. No more toward the scrow
I mount. Downsteepy is the pit below.
Ah, hadavist . . . a drumly, trantled chime.
My very outwit is malapropos:
Forgotten words are mighty hard to rhyme.

                    Envoy
The ghosts of blore and paggle past me blow—
The coverslut, the okselle, all *de trop.*

To lose straight-fingered phrases seems a crime.
Yet deep inside I cry, "Bravissimo!"—
Forgotten words are mighty hard to rhyme.

APPENDIX
Glossary of obsolete terms
in "Chantpleure"

Eldnyng: Jealousy, envy

Sloomy: Lazy, dull, sleepy

Chantpleure: Sing and weep simultaneously

Ha-ha: A sunk fence or ditch

Hadavist: Had I but known

Younghede: Youth

Abluscent: Cleansing, purifying

Chair day: Old age

Stoopgallant: That which humbles the great

Shab: Get rid of

Adush: Cause to fall heavily

Pitchkettle: Puzzle

Suggil: Beat black and blue, defame

Hoful: Cautious

Scantling: Scanty

Outwit: Knowledge

Thrip: A snap of the fingers

Cark: Care

Ribble: Wrinkle, furrow

Ycore: Chosen, elect

Boonfellow: Warm companion

Hum: A mixture of beer or ale and spirits

Aimcry: Encourage

Turngiddy: Drunk

Bashy: Thin, weak

Kill-priest: A strong drink

Eaubruche: Adultery

Fairhead: A beauty

Eyebite: Wink at

Donge: Bed

Draggle-tail: A wanton, prostitute

Fage: Coax, beguile, entice

Inwit: Conscience

Shittle: Unstable, inconstant

Bedswerver: An unfaithful husband

Housebreak: A home wrecker

Poop-noddy: A fool; also the game of love

Fonkin: A little fool

Bellibone: A dear, good, lovely maiden

Lip-clap: Kiss, kissing

Truehead: Fidelity

Fellow-feel: Empathize

Scrow: Sky

Frush: Crush, destroy

Mubblefubbles: Melancholy

Wong: Moor

Cockshut: Dusk

Croodle: Cheeping

Nesh: Fresh, young

Open-tide: Spring
Lennow: Flabby, limp
Spittle: Hospital for
    indigents, lepers, and the
    like
Samdead: Half-dead
Bell-penny: Money saved for
    one's funeral
Acclumsied: Physically
    impaired, paralyzed

Downsteepy: Precipitous
Drumly: Cloudy, sluggish
Trantled: Of little value
Blore: Cry or bray like an
    animal
Paggle: Bulge, hang loosely,
    as a belly
Coverslut: Apron
Okselle: Armpit
Straight-fingered: Honest

DICHOTOMY, TRICHOTOMY

(*The Times* [of London] *Higher Educational Supplement* reports the appearance of "trichotomy" as an erroneous definition for a division into three parts.)

In Greek, "apart" is dicha. Tomia
  Means "cutting." Thus, "dichotomy"
Means "something cut apart."
            Encomia
  To him who knows those severed parts can be
Of any number! Jeering to the one
  Who, holding di *in Greek's confined to "two,"*
Invents "trichotomy" if parts be three.
  In Greek, what's tricho? *"Hair." The simpleton*
Has coined a word for "haircut"! Or 'twould do
  For "splitting hairs." Both sound all right to me.

7

O GEE, ETTY!

A TICKLE and a slap, that is my relationship to Etty, my favorite among the goddesses. She was hailed respectfully as Etymology until the feminist movement liberated her; now she calls herself Etty, or, in naughty moments, Moll; I have been known to marvel in the small hours of the night, "O Etty! Moll! O Gee!"

Etty is gray-eyed and fair-skinned, quiet before the first drink, but willing thereafter to match glass for glass and story for story until her companion (never herself) blurs off into a happy stupor. Her formal name combines Greek *etymos*, "truth," with *-ology*, "science"; she provides her worshipers with orgiastic delights simply by showing them where words come from.

> The nicest thing that I can do
> For those I take a fancy to
> Is place them in the retinue
>   Of lovely Etty Moll O'Gee.
>
> She's mentor, muse, and mistress too,
> But only for the lucky few
> Who find the words they need to woo
>   My lovely Etty Moll O'Gee.

Asked to choose for high drama, breathless adventure, and uproarious laughter between a yarn spun off by Etty and such lesser works as, say, Plutarch's *Lives* or Shakespeare's *Taming of the Shrew,* I would plump for

Etty every time. The shenanigans of TV soap operas like *Dallas* never riveted me to my seat so tightly as do Etty's soap operas of word origins.

Now that Etty's consciousness has been raised, she likes to remind me that the words "male" and "female" have no common origin. *Femina* was Latin for woman, and *femella* for young woman; the latter word became "female" in English only because of an accidental similarity of sound.

Marijuana, a drug derived from the cannabis plant, has been plausibly assumed to combine Maria and Juana, girls' names in Spanish; our slang expression "Mary Jane" for cannabis echoes that assumption. But Etty says "marijuana" actually reflects Arabic *marjui*, "kneaded," from the fact that the plant was worked into cakes.

Even in her cups, Etty is elegant. Her sister, Folk Etymology, on the other hand, tends to go around with wrinkled dresses and tangled hair. Sister Folk traces the changes that occur in words through the usage of the common people, who have a habit of substituting what is easy to say for what has elegant precedence. Folk Etymology turned *muskmelong* into "mushmelon" and *asparagus* into "sparrowgrass." Folk reminds us that the Jerusalem artichoke is no artichoke, though it tastes like one, for "Jerusalem" corrupts *girasole*—Italian *girare*, "to turn," plus *sole*, "sun." The Jerusalem artichoke is only a sunflower. Rosemary, a shrub with pungent leaves and generally blue blossoms, is not a rose, nor is it named for the Virgin Mary; Latin *ros* is "dew," and *marinus* "of the sea"; the name is from the appearance of the plant, as fragile as sea-foam. The German word *Meerschaum* for a generally white mineral often used to make bowls of tobacco pipes is identical with "rosemary" in its origin; it comes from *Meer*, "sea," plus *Schaum*, "foam."

"Shamefaced," declares Folk, has no connection with "face." The word evolved from *scamfoest,* "held fast by shame." Nor did "hangnail" start as a bit of skin attached to a fingernail; the "hang" corrupts Old English *ange,* "painful," progenitor also of the word "anguish." As to the nail, it meant "a corn on the foot," a hard corn being likened to the head of a nail.

The first recorded ancestor of the goddesses Etty and her sister Folk is Etymon. Etymon, "the true word"— that is, the earliest known version—perished when, more than two thousand years before Christ, God confounded the tongues of men:*

EPITAPH FOR AN ETYMON

For Etymon I lay this wreath;
    He slipped his mortal cable
Four thousand years ago, beneath
    The shattered Tow'r of Babel.

But he left many children:

ON THE FERTILITY OF THE ETYMON

Dear Etymon, before you died,
    Suspecting how we'd miss you,
You spread your favors far and wide;
    The Cognates are your issue.

Cognates are words descended from a common ancestor—as Southerners say, 'kissin' kin.' Etymologists state, for instance, that ancient Sanskrit *vidua,* "empty," and modern English "widow" are cognate words; but like anthropologists seeking to connect apes with men, they have not yet been able to establish the missing link.

* See "The Ziggurat of Babel," page 235.

KISSING COGNATES

You're a dear, and I'm unbearable.
You look lovely; I look terrible.
You are kind and honest; I
Kick all helpless things, and lie.
Yet we're Cognates, kissing kin,
Common heirs to what has been.
In our genes the blood flows on
Of Great-grandpa Etymon.

Etty's cousin Metathesis is in charge of transposing letters and sounds as language evolves. In English, Metathesis turned the verb "ax" to "ask"; "bridd" to "bird"; "waeps" to "wasp"; "lips," the speech impediment, to "lisp"; "thridd" to "third." I sometimes try to persuade acquaintances that the name Espy is metathesized from Latin *episcopus*, "bishop."

Folks, metathesize my name—
    Rhyme it with the ads for Pepsi!
I give autographs to frame
    If you call me "Willard Epsy."

As I sat dozing, Etty wakened me by running her fingers through my hair. That is the way pleasures start, and I was ready; but Etty, who sometimes seems one part vixen to nine parts schoolmarm, drew back.

"Perhaps I'm not in the right humor," she told me.

"If you weren't, you would not be here," I pointed out.

"Ah—but *which* humor? There are four in the body, you know; one's mood at any instant reflects the balance among them."

"I know the four humors," I said. "They are the

cheerful *sanguine,* from Latin *sanguis,* 'blood'; the dull
phlegmatic, from Latin *phlegma,* 'body moisture'—the
clammy mucus that generates apathy; the angry *choleric,*
from Greek *chole,* yellow bile; and the mournful *melan-*
cholic, from Greek *melan,* 'black,' plus the same *chole*—
black bile. I am sure your dominant humor just now is
sanguine, my dear; you are filled with energy, good
cheer, amativeness. I can see by the color in your cheeks
that your blood is pounding, Etty."

"But no woman must let herself become too sanguine," she murmured, "or men will take advantage of
her. Think of poor Nell Gwynn, Charles II's mistress.
How betrayed she was—and yet how foolishly happy!
They used to sing in the London streets:"

> The King lyde Nelly down fer fun
>   To plarnt 'is byby in.
> Gwynn sang fer joy w'en 'e wuz dun;
>   The byby's nyme's "Sang Gwynn."

Here she let me touch her smooth white hand, and
even press it. But still she shook her lovely head in
doubt. "Perhaps I may be overcome by phlegm. Do I
seem phlegmatic, my dear?" She pursed her lips in a
pout and regarded me soberly from wide gray eyes.

My forefinger located the pulse of her inner elbow.
"Your heartbeat is quick," I said, "which cannot be from
phlegm. Besides, the Phlegms are humors of a low social
order; you would never have dealings with them:"

> Phlegm's pa was Fleming; Flemings are
>   Related to the Dutch.
> They're known for cheese and wooden shoes,
>   And don't amount to much.

"You are unkind and unfair to the Flemings," she
said; "they must be the cleanest people in the world,

and they *do* amount to much. But I agree that I am not phlegmatic." Here she noticed that I had begun to stroke the hollow of her elbow; she snatched her arm away. "But I warn you that I can be choleric—oh, yes, I can be choleric!" Lightning bolts shot from the gray clouds of her eyes. "Choler causes rage, as well as bilious attacks. It even causes the dread plague cholera itself. You made eyes at Folk when you thought I was not looking—haven't I reason to be in a rage with you?"

"Folk is a darling," I said, "but we both know she can never be a rival of yours. Your pulse reflects heat, to be sure, but anger is only one way of manifesting heat; it may break out in quite the opposite fashion:"

> What led to Choler's origin
>   Is known by fool and scholar;
> A nun grew hot beneath the skin,
>   A priest beneath the collar.

"Then I must be suffering from melancholy," she said, and drooped her head against my shoulder.

"Even if you are, it is not serious," I said, putting my arm around her. "Here, I will sing a song to cheer you up:"

> A dog and cantaloupe went sparking;
>   What issued from that folly?—
> A fruit that wagged its tail when barking;
>   They called it Melon Collie.

At that instant *a capella* voices rose invisibly about us. The words were sweet and clear:

> We humble humors slosh about
>   Inside your mortal sack;
> We're blood; we're phlegm; our bile comes out
>   Now yellow and now black.

You're *sanguine* when your blood flows hot;
    But when your phlegm takes over,
You're *dull* and *sluggish;* phlegm is not
    The humor for a lover.

Black bile breeds *melancholic* mood,
    While yellow bile breeds *choler.*
Folks ruled by yellow bile are rude,
    And execrations holler.

As the voices faded, Etty whispered into my shoulder, "Truly, I am melancholy tonight. It oppresses me that even words are mortal, and even the gods must die. Comfort me, my dear."

I comforted her.

MINIUM
(red lead, cinnabar; Latin)

In olden days, the Latin for red lead
  Was minium, *and monks used minium*
To intersperse dull manuscripts with red.
  So tiny were their paintings, mini's *come*
To mean not red in hue, but wee in size;
When you paint small, you min-i-a-tur-ize.

8

BIBLE BY COMMITTEE

Or, drat it, they're still at it.

"I REGRET, my good man," said James I, "that I need help to dismount."

He towered in my library, bestriding a roan stallion that I guessed a full fifteen hands in height. I hastily wished up some hay for the animal, and it leaned its head down to eat, the reins slack on its neck.

"I suffered throughout life," said James, groaning now as I took his hand and eased him off his mount, "from a weakness of the lower extremities, so that when I walked I required the shoulder of an attendant to lean on. I sometimes had to be tied to my saddle, so great was the weakness of my legs. But do not misunderstand me—I rode well, sir, I rode well. Your Buffalo Bill could not have done better."

I helped him arrange himself in my easiest chair.

"I know you despise tobacco," I said, "but I hope you will join me in a glass of wine. A stirrup cup, so to speak."

He accepted the wine with a gracious nod, drained it off, and handed back the glass for a refill.

"Had I not known you to be an abstainer from the hellish weed, sir," he said, "assuredly I would not have accepted your invitation to visit." As he spoke, his deep eyes flashed; the ruffle about his throat seemed to swell like the wattles of a fighting cock. "Should men not be ashamed, to sit tossing off tobacco pipe, and puffing of the smoke of Tobacco one to another, making the filthy smoke and stink thereof, to exhale athwart the dishes? It is a custom loathsome to the eye, harmful to the brain, dangerous to the lungs, and in the black stinking fume thereof, nearest resembling the horrible Stygian smoke that is bottomless." He tossed off his second glass of claret.

"I feel exactly the same way," I said, pouring him a third. "But there was another subject I hoped we might talk about. You were the man who ordered and supervised the King James Version of the Holy Bible. It is generally considered to be outstanding among Bibles. Some scholars consider it the finest work of literature in English. No later translations match it for clarity, and for loveliness of language. Yet a Committee prepared that Bible, Your Majesty; and everybody knows that committees are hopelessly incompetent. What made yours different?"

"In the first place," said James, "I set up not just one committee, but several, each covering a different section. They labored mightily, and the spirit of the Lord was with them. But I myself, sir, stood behind them with a pitchfork. It has been too little noted, sir, that I not only was King of Scotland and England (and that by divine right) but, also by the grace of God, was myself an author, surely unique since Alfred for the width of my intellectual interests. The King James Version of the Bible, sir, is not, as was its predecessor, a Bishops' Bible: it is my own creation."

He explained in detail, sipping more slowly now at his wine, how he had supervised his appointed scholars at their work. I did not drink with him, being too busy taking notes. He was still talking and I still scribbling hours later when the horse, having finished eating its hay, broke into a loud neigh.

"When he calls, I know it is time to go," said the King.

James had difficulty mounting the horse, whether because of the wine or because of his old infirmity I could not say, but he finally made it when I gave his buttocks a boost. He was swaying but erect in the saddle as horse and man faded from view.

A revised version of my notes follows.

Preamble

God didn't bother to hire a crew, not even an off-duty
   Archangel shooting craps with a dozing Cherubim
(No need of help for HIM!)
When he spent six days from morning till evening, ham-
   mering and sawing and tinkering and sewing, cob-
   bling together Day, Night, Heaven, Earth, Land,
   Sea, Plants, Sun, Moon, Stars, Fowl, Great Whales,
   Cattle, Creeping Creatures, Adam, and, from
   Adam's rib, Eve.
Several thousand years passed before anyone drew a
   moral from this divine tour de force; but finally a
   medieval Pundit leaped from bed one morning,
   clapped a hand to his forehead, and cried out in a
   loud voice, "Eureka! I have found it! I now perceive
The Story of Creation is an analogy informing mankind
   that the creative process, except in its procreative
   aspects, is meant to be a solitary exercise!" The
   Pundit then rushed to his desk, seized his quill pen,
   and scrawled that memorable ditty,
"No committee/Has Creative-itty."

   (Do not, however, confuse committeefication
   With collaboration—
   With Beaumont and Fletcher
   Deriding the lecher;
   With Kaufman and Hart
   Turning musical comedy into art;
   Or with the happy rat-a-tat upon an impenetrable skull
   Of Gil. and Sul.)

Canto I, in which
the Pundit's thesis
wins general acceptance

This medieval discovery was so apt, so profound, and indeed, even an itty

Bit witty

That the Pundit dined out on it for years, and might be dining out on it still,

If he had not had the mischance to perish through the mischance of falling ill.

But by then his epiphanous statement

Had become so embedded in our genes that it still bounces from generation to generation with no hint of abatement.

Whenever experts foregather to snap their choppers at some sinewy problem of morals or state or physics (sometimes masticating the subject in unison and sometimes in turns, passing it from one set of choppers to the next amid such pleasantries as "If you chance to bite down on a resistant sinew,

May it dissolve within you")—

Whenever that happens, there is bound to be a carper outside the window carping, "For goodness' sake, stop picking one another's brains! Be innovative!

You know perfectly well that no Committee ever created anything creative!"

This point of view is especially popular in the fraternity of Creative Art:

No musician would attend a symphony composed by a Committee, even a Committee composed of Beethoven, Brahms, Tchaikovsky, and Mozart.

If the Good Lord were to appoint Lipchitz and Rodin and Calder and Moore to a Committee

To design a new frieze for the portal to the Heavenly City,

The Redeemed would march as one on Saint Peter,
carrying thousands of scrolls with petitions to scrap
the frieze on account of it wasn't very pretty.
(A possible exception to the Pundit's dictum might be
those Renaissance workshops which produced
paintings attributed to "the School of So-and-So,"
since nobody can tell which painting was the work
of the apprentice and which of the master;
Though my guess is that the ones with the hastiest
brushstrokes are the master's, since he would know
how to paint faster.)

Yet there is no denying that the champion of all literary
works, the King James Version of the Bible, was
created by a Committee.
This is a great pity
And reflects unfavorably on the foresight of James I,
that puissant Prince,
For Committees, being harder to stop than to start, have
been writing worse and worse Bibles ever since.

Canto II, in which
King James gives the
Committee its
marching orders
Dwight Macdonald says the King James Version of the
Bible is probably the greatest translation ever
made, and John Livingston Lowes
Termed it the noblest monument of English prose,
And they may be right. But I do wish the project had
been the by-blow of one of your bohemian pot-
tossers,
One of your Bill Shakespeares or Bobby Burnses or
Geoff Chaucers,

If only because, being mortal, they could have found no
way of arranging things
To hang around forever changing things.
Instead, the historic enterprise originated with a "Com-
mittee of Scholars representing the contending
High Church and Low Church parties at Oxford,
Cambridge, and Westminster, convened by King
James I at Hampton Court Palace in January
1604," to decide why so many Christian voices were
out of pitch as they emulated the Heavenly Choir.
And if I am wrong in any jot or tittle of the foregoing,
then the Eleventh Edition of the *Encyclopaedia Bri-
tannica* is an unmitigated liar.
Now, these are the commands the Crown
Laid down:
*The Committee was to prepare a more accurate yet more majes-
tic translation than any of its predecessors; one as vernacular as that of the martyred Tyndale, who in the time of
Henry VIII had bragged of his unfinished Bible to a Cath-
olic prelate, "I wyle cause a boye that dryveth the plough
shall know more of the scripture than thou knowest"; yet
also one whence poured*
The full wildness and passion of the Lord.

*Canto III, which
names certain
Committee members
but ignores others*
When you get right down to the nitty-gritty,
The King James Bible was not created by a Committee:
it was created by a Committee within a Committee
within a Committee within a Committee.
Fifty-four scholars undertook this monumental task for
James. Some died along the way, others are lost; I'll
spare you all but a few of the names:
William Bedwell, the greatest Arabic scholar of Europe,
for instance; did he really bed well, or not?

Was he noted among his colleagues for begetting, or
    simply for being begot?
By name alone, John Overall should have headed the
    Committee, but I gather he wound up as Bishop of
    Norwich,
Eating cold plum porridge.
By name alone, such divines as Lively and Rabbit are
    bound to attract notice. Then there is Andrewes, to
    whom I shall refer later; and out of filial devotion
    I must mention one name more—
John Richardson, whom my mother used to claim as
    one of her bears-fore.
Of the list extant I can rhyme barely two,
And them only by accenting the second syllable of
    Harding to make it rhyme with Byng, which seems
    an ungentlemanly thing to do.

*Canto IV, which
divides by category
the tasks assigned
to the Subcommittees*

You may feel threatened nowadays by muggers or air
    pollution or mercury in swordfish or the chance
    that a truck may swing around the corner and hit
    you, but you don't know what a real menace is
Until you are tapped by your Sovereign to serve on a
    Subcommittee charged with making a fresh trans-
    lation out of the original tongues, with the former
    translations diligently compared and revised. Per-
    haps your special responsibility is to proceed to
    Kings, by way of Exodus, Leviticus, Numbers, Deu-
    teronomy, Joshua, Judges, Ruth, and Samuel, start-
    ing from Genesis;
Or to be one of those scholasties
Who break camp when the sun comes up over Chroni-
    cles, and ride camelback through Ezra and Ne-
    hemiah and Esther and Job and Psalms and

Proverbs until they settle down for the night at Ecclesiastes;

Or one of those who map every desert and oasis between Egypt and Canaan to lay a

Geographical and chronological pathway stretching all the way to Malachi (with rest stops at Jeremiah, Lamentations, Ezekiel, Daniel, Hosea, Joel, Amos, Obadiah, Jonah, Micah, Nahum, Habakkuk, Zephaniah, Haggai, and Zechariah) from Isaiah:

Or you may be assigned to the Apocrypha; or to come to grips

With Matthew, Mark, Luke, John, The Acts, and eventually Revelation, also called the Apocalypse;

Or even to join a Subcommittee of scholars so holy they are said not to notice whether they are dressed or nude—

An unimportant matter in the daylight, when their subject is Romans, but more provocative after nightfall, when they are dealing with something, or somebody, named Jude.

Canto V, in which
years pass,
and the great
Bible is born,
or ex-pressed

Once every Committee member had received his assignment, the Lord entered into these saintly men, and all tongues became unto them as one tongue,

Which was easiest with Dr. Andrewes, already familiar with Hebrew, Chaldee, Syriac, Greek, Latin, and ten other languages, and thus of Committee translators the chief among.

In patristic tongues also Dr. Andrewes was unrivaled.

(I guessed "patristic" might hark back to vanished countries whose languages had barely survivaled,

Until I reflected that *patria,* country, comes from *pater,*
father, and gambled that "patristic" might therefore pertain to the ancient Fathers of the Church.
I looked up my guess in the dictionary, and for the
first time that night
I was right.)

After some years' delay,
Largely occasioned by arguments about how to dig up
the three shillings a week the scholars insisted on
for pay,
The Committee at last got down to it, and labored full
sore:
Indeed, the final translation "cost the workemen, as
light as it seemeth, the paines of twise seuen times
seuentie two days and more";
Which means they experienced two years and nine
months of labor, prayer, and stress
Before, in *anno Domini* 1611, the King James Version of
the Holy Bible at last emerged from the womb, or,
more precisely, came off the press.

Canto VI, in which
Committees
spring up like
toadstools
Inasmuch as patient scholarship presumably renders
translations
More precise as time passes, it is reasonable that the
King James Bible should from time to time require
a few emendations.
Yet I can't help feeling (though I know no more about
translating the Bible than I do about playing the
saxophone)

That after arriving at its apogee in King James, the
Church should have let well enough alone.
But since human nature insists that if one Committee is
good, two should
Be twice as good,
And three, three times as good, and so on, it was foreor-
dained that the King James Bible should be chal-
lenged by rank upon rank of contenders, including
the English Revised Version, the American Stan-
dard Version, the New English Bible, the Revised
Standard Version, the Jerusalem Bible, the New
American Bible, Today's English Version, the Liv-
ing Bible, and now the Good News Bible. Each
complains to the next, as the whiting did to the
snail,
That you're treading on my tail:
The version today's Committee creates
Is the version tomorrow's Committee outdates.
This plethora of Biblical shepherds may be very well;
But they do seem to lead their flocks farther and farther
from the gates of Heaven and nearer and nearer to
the gates of Hell.
I should think the Committees succeeding the Committees succeeding the Committees would consider it
odd
That the harder they work at creating Heaven on earth,
the closer they seem to come to destroying the
Heaven of God.

Canto VII, consisting
of a few random examples
of alteration by Committee
Perhaps it indeed improves something or other
To change "Am I my brother's keeper?" to "Am I supposed to take care of my brother?"
Nor is "What profit hath a man of all his labour which
he taketh under the sun?" so with it as "You spend

your life working, and what do you have to show
for it?"

But in both instances I go for the first; the second, I
don't go for it.

The newest Bible of all, the "Good News," is by all reports impeccable in scholarship. Its creators believe
it is as up-to-date as today's newspaper, and will be
as avidly read;

But they seem to have forgotten that if you pick up
today's newspaper tomorrow, nothing is as dead.

With the Bible, as with a man or woman, cosmetic surgery

Can verge on perjury.

Yet perhaps the changes are improvements; you may
applaud them. There is no page without an example;

This scattering should be ample:

King James	*Good News*
The Lord is my shepherd; I shall not want.	The Lord is my shepherd; I have everything I need.
Dust thou art, and unto dust shalt thou return.	You were made from soil and you will become soil again.
To every thing there is a season, and a time to every purpose under the heaven.	Everything that happens in this world happens at the time God chooses.
Remember now thy Creator in the days of thy youth, while the evil days come not, nor the years draw nigh, when thou shalt say, I have no pleasure in them.	So remember your Creator while you are still young, before those dismal days and years come when you will say, "I don't enjoy life."
The wicked flee when no man pursueth.	The wicked run when no one is chasing them.

If the salt have lost his savour, wherewith shall it be salted?	If the salt loses its saltiness, there is no way to make it salty again.
Consider the lilies of the field, how they grow; they toil not, neither do they spin.	Look how the wild flowers grow; they do not work or make clothes for themselves.

Many scholars hail the Good News Bible; a few would
  even toss the King James Version into the trash can,
  and you may agree.
But don't count on support from me.

  Canto VIII, in which
  a new James reigns
I had meant to end this dissertation on a positive note
Reflecting the results of the 1976 Presidential vote.
The English language, I meant to say, may indeed have
  reached its ultimate when King James's Committee
  clothed the neck of the horse with thunder and
  exulted, "He saith among the trumpets, Ha, ha;
  and he smelleth the battle afar off, the thunder of
  the captains, and the shouting";
But the Committee was the instrument of James; should
  not some of the credit given the Scholars who set
  about the translating go to the Prince who set about
  the set-abouting?
For the Committee was the horse, and the Prince was
  the rider holding the reins.
Why not now, then, a new Committee of Scholars (at
  the White House, or perhaps at Plains)
Convened by the James of our day, a born-again Christian who departs from the earlier Prince of the
  same name

In that only his heart, not the girl in question, takes
   notice when he lusts after a dame.
Therefore let James VI, shepherd of these United
   States (VI, not I, for James Madison, James Mon-
   roe, James Polk, James Buchanan, and James Gar-
   field preceded him through the White House gates)
Instruct that Committee, drawn from the very best
   brains
Of Plains,

Plus blacks, gays, Chicanos, women, Aleuts, Inuits, Indians, other ethnics too numerous to mention, old
   people, young people, schoolteachers, public employees, private employees, businessmen, artists,
   and every abused minority,
To draw up a Bible to end all Bibles, this to be certified
   by James's own authority.
Then the lion will lie down with the lamb, and Adam
   with Eve, and we shall need no Valiums to calm us
For we shall have to comfort us James's Holy Bible of
   the Heavenly Promise.
Then any who have ceased to be believers will become
   believers once more in good sooth;
Doubt will vanish from our hearts as the Serpent from
   Eden. From that day forward the Bible can only tell
   the truth,
For it will be the Authorized Version of James of Plains
   (whose initials are J.C.); and James, as we know
(For he has told us so, and told us so, and told us so),
Will never, never lie to us, and there's an end on it.
You can depend on it.
That is the positive note I would have ended on—logi-
   cal, optimistic, and weighty;
But before I could complete my composition, King
   James of 1976 had been succeeded by King Ronald
   of 1980.

DIPLOMACY
(Greek *diplōma*, folded paper)

When messengers of state set out,
They place their orders in a fold.
Since none can know what none is told,
We're never sure beyond a doubt
What they are sent to lie about.

9

THE WARS OF
THE WORDS

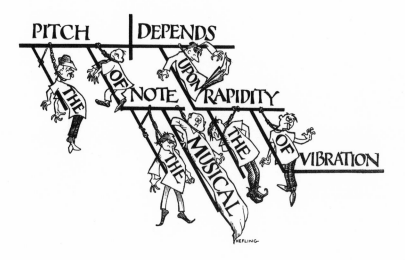

A gruesome memento.

SEVERAL shelves in the library of the house on Fifty-first Street are devoted to the development of the English language. First editions and rare books have a place there as a matter of course; they cost me nothing, since any volume that might interest me is instantly at my disposal. Of them all, I consider the most precious a tiny clothbound volume—less than half the size of a package of cigarettes—which I found one day in a desk drawer among a miscellany of rubber bands, correction fluid, staples, erasers, punches, paper clips, bottles of glue, and rolls of cellophane tape. I was unfamiliar with the title, nor was there any clue to the provenance of the book; the flyleaf lists neither the name of the author nor the year of publication. Yet *The War of the Words* is the most succinct and lucid account I have read of the stresses and strains that over the centuries have accompanied—and that continue to accompany—the ineluctable ebbs and flows of English usage.

It is a seminal work, a masterpiece of scholarship, and I reprint it here as a service to anyone who wishes to know just how our language arrived at its present state of perfection.

THE WARS OF THE WORDS

A royal peccadillo in the year of our Lord 1213 precipitated the Wars of the Words. King John was in the

Nominative case then, with many Subjects to do him honor. One of these Subjects—Matilda, daughter of Robert Fitzwalter the Valiant, Lord of the Manor of Diss in the County of Norfolk—discovered that she had also become the King's Object; and she Objected. The King responded by sending her "a messenger with a poisoned potched [*sic*] egg, whereof she died."

There ensued a wrangle among the Nouns. Could a Subject also be an Object? And how could one tell which was which? Some hearty old Nouns declared themselves loyal Subjects, and proud of it; others admitted they were Objects. They said any Subject that acted upon them would do so at his own risk. Words led to blows, blows to a pitched battle, and the battle to a carnage among Nouns more bloody than our own Civil War.

THE WARS OF THE NOUNS

Records of the first Wars of the Words are fragmentary, partly because it was difficult to separate who was fighting whom from whom was fighting who.

In the opening war, sometimes the Subjects were ahead, and sometimes the Objects. When the Objects triumphed, they became the Subjects, and the Subjects became the Objects. But this simply meant that they exchanged armor and went on fighting. To make the scoring still more difficult, a Subject that became an Object remained, or became, the Subject of its Subject.

The outcome was the Dark Ages. Armies degenerated into marauding bands. Father turned on son, and brother on brother. Split personalities were the norm. No one is sure how many centuries this chaos lasted. We do know, however, that finally an ancient Noun—his name has long been forgotten—climbed to the top of a beer barrel in the marketplace of Diss, drained his mug, and cried in a quavering voice, "This madness must cease. Whether Subjects or Objects, we are all Nouns together. We are the lords of creation—the First of the Parts of Speech—only a little lower than the angels. Who else, excepting only the oyster, can turn from Subject to Object and back again at will?"

From then on the Nouns were so busy and happy switching from Subject to Object and back again that they had no time or stomach left for fighting.

THE WARS BETWEEN
THE NOUNS AND THE VERBS

The Golden Age of Grammar dates from the Beer Barrel Speech. Sadly, like the Golden Age of Pericles, it could not endure; and for the same reasons: it was built upon the abominable system of slavery. Nouns were the masters; Verbs, Second of the Parts of Speech,* were the slaves. It was the nature of Nouns to *name* things, and of Verbs to *do* things, though as little as possible. Verbs were frequently wrenched from their families and sold at auction; infant *do*s were torn from the arms of their weeping *don't*s, and *won't*s from their little *will*s.

Sporadic uprisings among the Verbs were put down without mercy, until one night the inevitable happened: the Verbs burst forth as one from their hovels and slaughtered the unsuspecting Nouns in their beds. It was believed at first that not a Noun had escaped. It happened, however, that a considerable number of them had been spending the night in beds other than their own. From the windows of Pronouns, Adjectives, Adverbs, Prepositions, and other subordinate Parts of Speech, the Nouns escaped in their nightshirts to rally against the rebels.

* Verbs always insisted that *they* were the First of the Parts of Speech.

It would take blind Homer with his lyre to re-create the epic struggle that followed. The fighting was almost as amorphous as in the earlier Wars of the Nouns. If a Verb mastered his own Master, he would declare himself a Nominative, while the former Nominative might be at one time a Verb and at another an Object. The winners were the losers, and the losers the winners.

Both sides maintained retinues of retainers and hangers-on. In most cases, though, these did not amount to much: they spent most of their time carousing at the Rose or the King's Garter, or playing unrecorded games with the village wenches. They considered a fight something to avoid. It took a sharp-eyed Noun or Verb to tell whether the mailed horseman charging him was an enemy or simply one of his own followers heading prudently for the neutrality of the backwoods, where nobody cared whether a plural Noun bedded with a singular Verb or the other way around.

PRONOUNS

The Pronoun was the one servitor upon whom a Noun could rely with confidence. A Pronoun would unhesitatingly step into the path of an arrow aimed at his Noun, or fight on if the Noun decided, say, to take a nap in a haycock or spend an hour rubbing his back against a tree. Major battles were waged by Pronouns while their Nouns relaxed in the great halls of their castles, swigging down mead and roaring out war songs. But Nouns became nervous about pronouns when scientists discovered that for every Pro-noun in the universe there must exist, for the sake of symmetry, an equivalent Anti-noun. If ever the two meet, the result will be instant and total annihilation. Since this discovery, Nouns have been sidling away from their Pronouns, and furtively slipping Adjectives in between.

ADJECTIVES

It is the function of an Adjective to *limit:* a *weak* man is not a *strong* man; a *cowardly* man is not a *brave* man. One of the first concerns of any Noun leaving for war was to surround himself with whatever Adjectives would best protect him, while locking up the rest in the castle dungeon.

But Adjectives are escape artists. Again and again a Noun would be joyously swinging his broadsword, safe in a phalanx of reassuring Adjectives like Stout and Victorious and Triumphant, when who should come barking over the hill but those very Adjectives he had safely stowed away for the duration—Nervous, and Uncertain, and Purblind, and Apprehensive—all eager to fawn on him, lick his face, trip him by running between his feet, and jump up and catch his best-shot arrows in midair.

ADVERBS

The Adverb was the only retainer whose sympathies lay with the Verb rather than the Noun. But while he was perfectly happy modifying a Verb, he was no less happy modifying an Adjective, or even another Adverb. He was incorrigibly promiscuous.

The nature of the problem is hinted at in this ancient poem, transcribed from a manuscript smuggled out to me by the head sweeper of the Bodleian Library:

ALLE IN YE FAMILY

Behinde a door with figne "Do not difturbe,"
An Adiective, two Adverbes, and a Verbe,
Each wedded to ye other three, debate

How quartets coniugal fhould coniugate.
Ye Adverbes tofs a penny to decide
Who'll Modify, and who be Modify'd.

As Groome, ye winning Adverbe willing lies
With Verbe and Adiective; but when he plies
His blandifhments on Adverbe, all's in vaine
Till he agrees to tofs ye coin again.
Head now turns Tail: each Adverbe's Groome; each, Bride;
Each, Modifier; and each, Modify'd.

(Whatever ftate Grammatical they're in,
Inceftuoufly fpeaking, they're in fin.)

PREPOSITIONS

The Preposition shows *relationship*. Prepositions come
in many kinds and degrees: *father, mother, son, daughter,
uncle, aunt,* and so on. Both Nouns and Verbs sought to
maintain cordial and correct relationships with their
Prepositions. They did not always succeed, as may be
seen from the instance cited here:

A PAIR IN CATS

A pair in cats, a Tom and Puss,
The parents with a pair in kits,
Among each other had a fuss,
Which ended down since snarls till spits.

The matter under which they fought,
At least to which I am aware,
Regarded toward a mouse they'd caught,
Through who should have the larger share.

Tom mentioned for his Pussy Cat,
At manner not polite with tone,
Her close resemblance from a bat—
She clawed his jaw aboard the bone.

So in and in the battle went. . . .
What happened meanwhile up the mouse?
When Tom and Puss were close by spent,
It left, and now stays safe to house.

Both Nouns and Verbs had the sagacity to follow the one rule about Prepositions that must never be violated. It is: Always use them to end sentences with. The only tolerable violation of the rule is to end a sentence with *more* than one preposition.

PARTICIPLES

Sometimes a Participle would show up for battle wearing the helmet and cuirass of a Verb, and the bra-connières and greaves of an Adjective. Sometimes he appeared to be all Adjective; sometimes all Noun. To be blunt about it, Participles were not trustworthy allies.

INFINITIVES

It is painful to report that even Verbs, whose very existence was at stake in their war with the Nouns, could be bribed into treason. All that was necessary was for some Noun to offer them membership in the ancient order of To-Whit To-Who. The suborner would place the flat of his sword on the shoulder of the Verb—say, a Mr. Run—and pronounce, "I dub thee *To*." Once dubbed *To* Run, he was addressed as "You Too" till the end of his days. He also enjoyed such other perquisites as the right to wear his hat in the presence of the King.

To-verbs were called Infinitives, from the Latin for "without limit." An Infinitive could change at will from Noun to Adjective to Adverb. The Infinitive was therefore in great demand by both Nouns and Verbs, and could name his own price.

INTERJECTIONS

Only Interjections took no sides in the Wars of the Words. They considered these purely spectator sports. They sat in the bleachers and shouted, "Hurray!," "Oh!," "Ah!," "Pooh!," "Pshaw!," "Bah!," "Ahoy!," "Fap!," "Gorblimey O'Reilly!," and so on, depending on whether the side they had bet their ha'pence on was running ahead or behind.

PARSING

Under the chaotic circumstances I have described, it is not surprising that the normal courtesies of war eventually broke down. The Hague Convention was ignored; whoever caught an enemy defenseless, slew him. Battles became euphemisms for lynching bees; the winners left the losers dangling from fence rails and tree branches, supper for a carrion crow. These dead were described as *parsed;* that is, they had *parsed* on to a better world. In my researches I was fortunate enough to find back of the stag's head in the trophy room of a decayed Cotswold castle a steel engraving of such a parsing (reproduced on facing page)—a gruesome memento of some forgotten victory.

MORAL

Sheer exhaustion finally put a period to the Wars of the Words. We still hear of an occasional byre's being burned down. Verbs in their rags still mutter obscenities when Nouns canter past in their panoply. But for the nonce all is quiet on the grammatical front. I do not

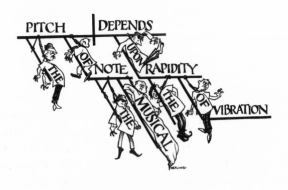

A gruesome memento

know what may be abrew behind the calm—what mad genius of a Verb may be concocting an atomic bomb from the clinkers in his coal furnace; what Jack the Ripper of a Noun may be slinking through the streets at night in search of some lovely Verb to disembowel. Nor do I wish to know. I live, as I advise you to, by Espy's Law: *The less you know, the safer you are.*

COLLATION
(Latin *collatio,* a bringing together)

(In the fifth century, readings from Johannes Cassianus's *Conferences of the Fathers—Collationes Patrium—*were customary in monasteries. On fast days a light meal was served after the *collatio.* The meal came to be called a "collation"—a term later applied to any light repast.)

> *When monks and hermits took a crack*
> *At cultural collation,*
> *They often downed a pleasant snack*
> *By way of peroration.*
> *Words have a way of changing tack:*
> *We say "collation" now for "snack."*

10

DR. JOHNSON
COMES TO CALL

" 'A camelopard,' he quoted slowly . . ."

$\mathbf{D}$R. JOHNSON, it having come to his attention that I had been making rhymes on certain of his dictionary definitions, came calling, giving as excuse "It is my clean-shirt day." He was a big man, wig askew, his flesh flowing shapelessly under wrinkled clothes. His voice was loud, and his eyes bright blue. I settled him in a rocking chair, placed a quart of tea at his elbow, and expressed my honor at the visit. He replied, jerking his head in a bow:

"I look upon every day to be lost, in which I do not make a new acquaintance, particularly now that I have left mortality behind."

Still, I said, it was a long way to come to look at a handful of doggerel.

"Mean, despicable, worthless verses such are," he agreed. "Still, Sir, every man's affairs, however little, are important to himself, and why should his doggerel be excluded? Besides, I am at the point where it flatters me to have the attention of one living. Flattery, Sir, is a rare commodity in eternity. The difference between me and Sam Richardson was that much flattery always disgusted me.* Richardson, on the contrary, could not be contented to sail quietly down the stream of his reputation, without longing to taste the froth from every stroke of the oar."

* Samuel Richardson wrote *Pamela: or, Virtue Rewarded,* regarded as the first modern English novel.

"I would like," I said, "to write about how English has changed since your dictionary was published in 1755. You have no entry, for instance, under the letter X. You say, 'X is a letter which, though found in Saxon words, begins no word in the English language.' "

"The statement was correct," he said.

"Still, you must have known about Xanthos, the wonderful horse of Achilles; Xantippe, wife of Socrates; St. Francis Xavier, the great Jesuit missionary; Xenophon, the Greek historian; and above all, Xerxes, the Persian king of kings."

"Mine was not a dictionary of biography. Even Shakespeare is not entered."

I was out first time at bat.

"But if you have a verse on my omission of X, Sir," he continued graciously, "pray let me hear it. A poetaster is indeed a vile petty fellow; but Parnassus has its flowers of transient fragrance, as well as its oaks of towering height and its laurels of eternal verdure; and no doubt God loves them all. Read, Sir; read on."

He drained off a cup of steaming tea at a gulp, spilling a few drops into the saucer. I refilled his cup, and read:

> Dr. Johnson laid a hex
> On th' initial letter X.
>   (Xceptionally
>   Xenophobic he,
> Though he'd never heard
> Of that xcellent word!)
>   He x'd from his workses
>   All x's, e'en Xerxes.
> Johnson never would have picked
> Xmas for his famous Dict.
>   His teeth decayed
>   Un-x-rayed.
> I think he would have hated
> Films marked "x-rated."

"It is currish doggerel indeed," said Dr. Johnson. "But let us not quarrel over that. You err, however, if you think that lewd spectacles comparable to your pornographic films were unfamiliar in the eighteenth century. I frequently beheld for no charge as I strolled through Covent Garden performances that doubtless would be classified XXX-rated today, with tickets going at several dollars apiece."

"You were congratulated for keeping lascivious references out of your dictionary."

"The credit may be undeserved. After all, I had reached my middle years by the time I compiled it. Our tastes, Sir, greatly alter with age. The lad does not care for the child's rattle, and the old man does not care for the young man's whore."

Here his gross countenance came alight; his wide mouth stretched wider; such a fit of laughter choked off his words that he appeared to be almost in a convulsion. At last he went on, between gasps and chuckles:

"Two gentle ladies once much commended me for those omissions. 'What, my dears!' said I—'then you have been looking for them!'"

I smiled. "Nobody doubts that you liked women."

"Had I had no duties, and no reference to futurity, I would have spent my life in driving briskly in a post-chaise with a pretty woman, sir; now that I am dead, my regret is that I so indulged myself too seldom. I appreciate the endearing elegance of female friendship. Yet the ladies do tend toward the hypocritic; they know they stir one wickedly. I had to cease visiting behind the scenes of David Garrick's plays, so did the silk stockings and white bosoms of his actresses excite my amorous propensities. Yet," he added reflectively, "they were wretched un-idea'd girls."

"Do you remember," I asked, "that you cited Dutch *bulcke*—'the breast, the largest part of a man'—as the source of our 'bulk,' meaning 'magnitude, size, quantity'? My Aunt Dora would have added 'woman' to the definition. She always called any particularly Junoesque female 'a fine, upstanding, double-breasted woman.' If she had had her way, Edgar Allan Poe would have written:"

> Thy bulk of double breast to me
> Like those Nicean barks of yore
> That gently, o'er a perfumed sea,
> Bore wanderers to shore—
> Like some inflated sugar plum
> In sweetness, swell and span
> Bears gently to its destined home
> The central part of man.

"You have some remarkably succinct definitions," I said, "in your dictionary. Weather, for instance, as 'state of air, respecting either cold or heat, wet or driness.' Laughter as 'convulsive merriment; an inarticulate expression of sudden merriment.' Those definitions say it all. But some words have expanded since your day. I've noticed that you define 'cosset,' for instance, only as 'a lamb brought up without a dam.' Nowadays it has come to mean any pet. It is also a verb for 'fondle':"

> I swore I would cosset my cosset, my lamb,
> And cherish her long as I live.
> She answered, 'I'm sorry—I don't give a dam;
> I haven't a dam, sir, to give.'

"I am the last to sneer at a pun," said Dr. Johnson, "but your example reminds me that the word first meant an empty sound, like that of a mortar beaten. Similarly, 'clench,' the old word for pun, seems only a corruption of 'clink.' "

"Dictionaries these days," I said, "define 'pun' as 'a fine point,' from Latin *punctum*, 'a pricked hole.' I have

written a verse that combines our present-day deriva-
tion with yours:"

> "Pun" comes, say scholars who should know,
> From *punctum*—pricked. "Punctilio,"
> "Punctilious," and "punctuate"—
> These too did *punctum* generate.
> Yet "pun" means too to "grind with Pestle
> In Mortar, or some other Vessel."
> "Clink, clench," cries Mortar as you pound;
> This pun denotes an empty sound.
> If barley into flour I pun
> To bake a cake for Honey-bun,
> The sounds you hear of clink and clench
> Are grateful kisses of my wench,
> Rewards for cake—sounds empty all
> As puns, and as equivocal.

"Wit, I suppose," said Dr. Johnson . . . "at a certain
level."

"I doubt," I said, "whether even low wit bothers you.
Fanny Burney said you had more love of fun and nonsense about you than almost anybody she ever saw."

"Humor is the highest of the defensive processes,"
said Dr. Johnson, "and verbal nonsense is at worst a
shirt-tail relative. I have written nonsense verse myself:"

> If the man who turnip cries
> Cry not when his father dies,
> 'Tis a proof that he had rather
> Have a turnip than his father.

"You also wrote," I reminded him:

> As with my hat upon my head
> I walked along the Strand
> I there did meet another man
> With his hat in his hand.

We talked for a while about the joys of nonsense, and then about popular words of Dr. Johnson's day that have mysteriously vanished—"grum" for "sour"; "mazy" for "perplexed"; "porwigle" for "tadpole." What destroyed them? Neither of us had any idea. And what changed the meaning of other words? Why does "salvo," for instance, no longer mean an "exception," though "save" still means "excepting that"?

"Sometimes," I said, "the old meaning remains, like a vermiform appendix. Take the word 'job.' You were contemptuous of it."

"Indeed," he said. "A low word, unfit for the mouth of a gentleman. A job is a low, mean lucrative affair— petty, piddling work."

"We still use the word unfavorably in one sense only," I said—"to 'job' someone, or 'to pull a bank job,' meaning 'to rob a bank'; but to hold down a job nowadays is essential to our self-respect—not to mention our livelihood. For women and men alike, 'job' is good; 'no job' is bad. We've got to work whether we like it or not:"

> Blob, glob, slob, rob—
> These rhyme with *job,*
> And right enough—
> Jobs are low stuff.
> (As smirk and shirk
> Rhyme with *work.*)

"You will stop a dog from barking, Sir," said Dr. Johnson, "before you will stop a word from changing its meaning when the time comes. It was in the mind of Dryden in the seventeenth century to found an institution for the regulation of English, after the example of the French Academy, and indeed he gathered much support. But then he died, poor man, and though Swift

154

continued to urge the proposal, it could not withstand the accession of George the German to the throne in 1714. George cared too little for English to learn it properly himself, much less impose order on it. But I for one regret the lack of an English Academy no more than your horse regrets that your cow miscarried. I would rather our speech were copious without order, and energetic without rules, than suspended forever unchanging, like a dead fly in gelatine. Sounds are too volatile and subtile for legal restraints; may the lexicographer be derided who shall imagine that his dictionary can embalm the language!"

"Would you defend plain mistakes too?"

"I would deplore them; but indeed I would argue that no mortal man is perfect."

"Do you recall your definition of a camelopard?"

"A camelopard," he quoted slowly, "is an Abyssinian animal, taller than an elephant, but not so thick. He is so named, because he has a neck and a head like a camel; he is spotted like a pard, but his spots are white upon a red ground. The Italians call him *giaraffa*."

"I have put your definition to rhyme:"

> The Camelopard, of an
> Order Abyssinian,
> Is, though a more taller fella,
> Lesser thicker than the ele-
> Phant. He's *camel*, neck and head—
> *Pard* below, white spots on red.
> Hence the name. But this here mammal
> Ain't no leopard, ain't no camel.
> An Italian, he would laugha:
> Camelopard's a *giaraffa*.

"Your first couplet doesn't rhyme; 'of an' and 'Abyssinian' are identicals."

"You're right. But you are wrong in your description. The coat of the camelopard is not red spotted with white, but tan spotted with brown. And the Italian name has taken over—we now call the beast a giraffe."

"Dictionaries are like watches," said Dr. Johnson, pouring himself more tea; "the worst is better than none, and the best cannot be expected to go quite true."

"Then it doesn't bother you," I said, "that you called a garret a room on the highest floor of the house, after defining a cockloft as a room over the garret?"

"Indeed it does," he said, "but I comfort myself that few accomplishments, even those of error, are impossible to diligence and skill. Moreover, I find any mistake in favor of the cock forgivable. He is a fowl remarkable for gallantry, pride, and courage. On balance, my definition of 'cockloft' is less error than exaggeration; and some exaggeration must be forgiven."

"I am being picky and presumptuous," I said, contrite. "Dr. Johnson, you must be floating in tea. Will you join me in something stronger?"

"Abstinence, Sir, is easy to me; temperance is more difficult. Yet I should be glad of a glass of claret. No, wait—claret is the liquor for boys, port for men, brandy for heroes. Let us be heroic tonight."

The brandy appeared on command, and we sipped. He gave his middle a contented pat, and remarked, "I look upon it, Sir, that he who does not mind his belly will hardly mind anything else."

"In your day," I said, "people took pride in their bulging waistlines. Now bulges terrify us."

He smothered a yawn with his hand. "The word is, after all, simply 'bilge.' And though 'bilge' is from Saxon *bilig,* 'bladder,' it stands for the lower part of the ship, where it swells out. There is nothing offensive about that."

"Again, though," I said, "there has been a change in point of view. 'Bilge' to me means the *contents* of the lower part of a ship, and they stink. We say of a ridiculous remark, 'Oh, bilge!' "

> By bilge and bulge
> Do I divulge
> The measure of my self-indulging:
> By bulging skin;
> By bilge therein;
> Within the bilge, by bloated bladder bulging.

There was no reaction (indeed, Dr. Johnson appeared to be drowsing), but I went on:

"Do you recall your definition of 'windward'?"

He shook his head to clear it, and replied, " 'Toward the wind.' "

"And how did you define 'leeward'?"

" 'Toward the wind' also."

"So a sailor, following your definitions, might find it hard to decide which way to come about."

"Experience and common sense will tell him," said Dr. Johnson; "he will not take my dictionary to sea. Do not expect perfection of a lexicographer, Sir. He is, after all, but a harmless drudge, that busies himself in tracing the original, and detailing the signification of words."

"You made so few mistakes that you can afford to smile at them, and I had no business bringing them up. Anyhow, what interests me most is what we were discussing before—the way words shift in meaning over the years. 'Senile' is a good example."

"In my time its meaning was plain enough: 'belonging to old age; consequent on old age.' Boyle used it with precision: 'My green youth made me very unripe for a talk of that nature, whose difficulty requires that it be handled by a person in whom nature, education, and time have happily matched a *senile* maturity of judgment with a youthful vigor of fancy.' "

"Yet today we associate senility with deterioration. We turn Boyle's kinship between wisdom and age inside out:"

> Ahead, calm harbor of senility
> Where mind matured joins youthful energy.
> Time, nature, education, match; all fits—
> Or would, but for concurrent loss of wits.

Dr. Johnson hid another yawn.

"Forgive me!" I exclaimed. "I am keeping you up; you're tired, and I am sure you have a full day tomorrow."

"No," he said, and his voice was dull; "tomorrow I purpose only to regulate my room. Tomorrow—and throughout eternity. For now, I would rather be here."

"No, I mustn't keep you any longer. But before you go, I'd like to recite just one more verse. It's about the word 'culprit.' In your time I gather it meant someone charged with a crime, correctly or not. Today it means an apprehended criminal."

"At one time," said Dr. Johnson, "a judge at criminal trials, when the prisoner declared himself not guilty, would answer, 'Culprit, God send thee a good deliverance.' The word is a likely corruption of *Qu'il paroit,* 'May it so appear'—the wish of the judge being that the prisoner may be found innocent."

"I prefer your meaning to ours," I said. "Here is the verse:"

> When I, poor Culprit, face the Lord of Law
> Who weighs my sins against His sufferance—

When to my plea he answers, *Qu'il paroit!* —
God send me then a good deliverance!

But the good ugly old man was fast asleep, lightly snoring. I leaned over and kissed his forehead.

"God bless you, my dear," I said.*

---

* These were Johnson's last words, spoken to a young lady who insisted on seeing him on his deathbed in order to ask his blessing.

EXCHEQUER.

The department of state concerned with revenue. (Medieval Latin *scararrim,* chessboard.)

> *Squares mark the chessboard-checkerboard.*
> *So marked the table is*
> *Where treasurers count up their hoard*
> *And do their money biz.*
>
> Exchequer's *named for chessboard; still,*
> *It's table less than trough;*
> *Hog shoulders hog; with snout in swill,*
> *They swig my taxes off.*

11
SAY NOW SHIBBOLETH

Les chemises de l'archiduchesse . . . ces six saucissons-ci . . . tres tristes tigres.

T HE trouble with Peter Piper was that he was so pleased with himself. Again and again he recited rapidly, and accurately:

Peter Piper picked a peck of pickled peppers.
Did Peter Piper pick a peck of pickled peppers?
If Peter Piper picked a peck of pickled peppers,
Where's the peck of pickled peppers Peter Piper picked?

Then he would roll his eyes at me as if to say, "*You can't do that.*"

I considered this disrespectful. I am a man of mature years, and Peter, from his appearance the evening he came to visit me, was snatched into immortality at about the age of twelve. Twelve-year-olds should not lord it over their elders and betters. So I decided to take him down a peg. I handed him a sheet of paper bearing the line

Szczerze czy wstrzemięźliwy szczodrze odziedziczył.[9]

"Read it aloud," I said.
"Read it? I don't even know what it means."
"Read it anyway."
He tried, I'll say that much for him. But his *s*'s became *z*'s, his *c*'s became *s*'s, and his *z*'s became *c*'s. Finally he said, "I give up. What is this silly thing?"

"It is a tongue twister in Polish, meaning 'The sincerely sober teetotaler inherited generously.' "

"How are you supposed to pronounce it?"

"I have no idea."

"That's not *fair.*"

"It is just as fair as your showing off because you know a tongue twister that you have been practicing ever since you could talk."

He brightened. "But I do know that one," he said, and began again:

"Pepper Piter pit a pep of pittled peckers . . ."

He couldn't get it. I smiled at him broadly, and he dashed from the room in a fury, shouting,

"If Peeker Kiper pip a kek of kittled teppers . . ."

My interest in foreign-language tongue twisters began—though I was not yet aware of it—when I was going on four. My brother, Edwin, senior to me by two years, asserted that millions of people throughout the world did not communicate through words, as we did, but instead spoke gibberish, pretending it meant something. My sister Mona, then aged eight or nine, replied with scorn that intelligible languages existed in abundance.

I leaned toward Edwin's view. Corporeal evidence favoring Mona's was available, however, immediately at hand, in my tiny home community of Oysterville, Washington. The evidence consisted of half a dozen remnants of the vanishing Chinook and Chehalis Indian tribes, known as Siwashes, after the French word *sauvage,* for "savage." All were old, closing in on their final accounting with the Great Spirit. Two were piratelike: one wore a peg below his right knee; the second flaunted a black patch over the empty socket of his right eye.

Though Indian powwows might sound like gibberish to us, Mona pointed out, clearly they meant something to the Indians. But I discounted this argument, since at times I could understand their conversation myself. The Chinook jargon had absorbed many familiar English words—"bed," "boat," "dolla," "house," "lazy," "man," "mama," "papa," "shoes," "smoke," "spose" (suppose). Moreover, my own childish vernacular included several Indian expressions—*skookum* for "first-rate"; *muckamuck* for "the evening meal"; *potlatch* for "gift." I was able to argue, therefore, that my friends were merely speaking a corrupt form of English. Anyhow, what could one learn about language from decrepit old men who usually did not speak at all, but only grunted?

Though I finally had to admit that Mona's argument bested Ed's, I confronted no foreign language myself (Chinook excepted) until my ninth year. The language was Latin, and my introduction to it coincided with my dazzling discovery of the mysterious magnetic pull of the complementary sex.

I spent more time those days with books than with people, and more time with people than with girls, a different species. But though our home library, sizable for our isolated location, was restricted in general to highly edifying reading matter, it was inevitable that a few racy volumes—*The Decameron, Cupid and Psyche, The Golden Ass*—should worm their way into the apple, and I was quick to follow the wormholes (or rather, to race through the books, as one should through racy tales) only to be blocked each time, just as the lovers were getting down to cases, by an abrupt shift from English into Latin. I could never confirm what Cupid and Psyche really *did*.

Like many of our family books, these were hand-me-downs from the nineteenth century, a period when it was in vogue to hide salacity in Latin. The rationale for this still escapes me. Did the publishers feel that Latin purified and exalted acts that would be too offensive for description in English? Or that anyone who had conquered Latin declensions and conjugations surely could beat back carnal temptation? Or perhaps, following a different line of thought, that such a demonstration of lingual skill deserved a reward beyond the ordinary?

In any event, I was left with no choice but to learn Latin; and learn Latin, after my fashion, I did, to the gratification of my father, who had once taught it. He drilled me in grammar and vocabulary, unaware that I was exploiting him to abet my lustfulness.

It turned out that the dark passages, once illuminated, said nothing more or less than I had suspected all along; but my prurience was increasing geometrically as I approached adolescence, and it became an article of faith to me that Ovid, Virgil, Martial, Juvenal, Catullus, and their fellow Romans *must* have recorded on yellowing parchment still more detailed descriptions of still lewder acts.* It was incumbent on me to reveal these hidden places. But at the last minute, what did those ancient writers do, as red-faced as their nineteenth-century successors? They vaulted—in the blink of an eye, faster than Proteus could change from a sea lion into a serpent—from classical Latin into classical Greek! At this point I had to concede that I was chasing a will-o'-the-wisp. I decided to confine my reading of Latin to seals of state.

Dabbling in Latin failed to make me a linguist, but it

---

* My prurience had its opposite among some Victorian Latinists. The great John Conington, for instance, concluded that his texts of Juvenal were irretrievably garbled in places where they described sexual amusements of which Conington had never heard.

served to strengthen the curiosity about languages and language sounds that had been awakened in me that day in my fourth year when I heard my brother and sister disputing whether the local Indians were talking sense or gibberish. So I became an instant addict a while back when a friend* handed me a piece of paper on which he had written: "*À Rocquevaire, la rivière se verse vers les verres du ver vert*"[1]—that is to say, "At Rocquevaire, the river flows toward the glasses of the green worm." This was a passage "*à décrocher la machoire, ou délier la langue*"—a passage to unhook the jaw, or untie the tongue! In a word, a *French* tongue twister!

In an epiphanic flash, Pei and "*À Rocquevaire*" knew each other (Biblically) in my mind. Thought I, "Of course! It stands to reason that since there are English tongue twisters, other languages must have them too. And tongue twisters in any language are as irresistible as peanuts—magical in their sound, magical in their senselessness. Moreover, when one stumbles in repeating them, as is inevitable, everybody laughs, including oneself.

"What a fascinating introduction to English pronunciation it would be," I told myself, "if foreigners were first drilled in 'She sells seashells at the seashore,' or 'The sixth sick sheik's sixth sheep's sick'! And if that applies to learning English, why not to learning other languages too?

"I have the cure," I cried aloud, "to the decline in foreign-language studies that is shattering the nerves of our pedants! A bare fifth of our high school students are exposed to any language but their own, and the

* The first contributor of each tongue twister in this chapter is identified by number, as follows: 1) Peter Prescott; 2) Mrs. David O. Tyson; 3) Paul Gaeng; 4) Anthony E. Bonner; 5) Mario Pei; 6) Arnold Perlman; 7) Richard Edes Harrison; 8) Robert Bendiner; 9) Brooks Wright; 10) Aira Neace; 11) Yukie La Pierre Ochiishe.

number is dropping every year, but I'll lure those students into polylinguality with bait they can't resist—tongue twisters!"

When the Gileadites, who spoke what they considered standard Hebrew, went to war with the Ephraimites, whose accent was barbarous to Gileadite ears, the Gileadites would demand of a suspected enemy:

> Art thou an Ephraimite? If he said, Nay; Then said they unto him, Say now Shibboleth; and he said Sibboleth: for he could not frame to pronounce it right. Then they took him, and slew him. . . .*

The Sicilians, revolting against the French usurpers of their island, ordered suspects to say *"Cicero ceci"* ("Cicero chick-peas"; Cicero had a wart like a pea on his nose). The expression requires four *ch* sounds in rapid succession. French prisoners, whose nation had given up the *ch* sound for the *sh* sound, tended to lapse into *sh* somewhere along the way; "and this," Professor Pei told me, "was too bad for them."

Some single words are tongue twisters. The longest Spanish word, *anticonstitucionalísimamente* ("most unconstitutionally"), trips even Spaniards if they say it fast enough.

Try pronouncing Czech *vrh pln mlh* ("a hill full of fog"); or Serbo-Croatian *Trst* (Trieste). The catch here is that in Czech and Serbo-Croatian, *l* and *r* function as vowels. Try also Polish *Grzeszczyszyn* (a family name); or Hawaiian *Kaliilikalakalakekeikiokuanaoa* (the nickname of a politician; I don't know what it means); or Hungarian *megbetegedetteknek* ("for those who became/are sick").

* Judges 12:5–6. *Shibboleth* means "ear of corn," "source," "flood."

Twisters from twelve tongues, often involving puns:

FRENCH

Les chemises de l'archiduchesse
Sont sèches et archisèches.[2]

("The archduchess's shirtwaists/Are dry and more than
dry.")
Un chasseur sachant chasser chassait un chat.[2] ("A hunter,
knowing how to hunt, hunted a cat.")
Didon dîna, dit-on, du dos d'un dodu dindon.[3] ("Dido
dined, they say, off the back of a plump turkey.")
La pipe au papa du Pape Pie pue.[3] ("The pipe of Pope
Pius' father stinks.")
Ces six saucissons-ci sont six sous les six.[3] ("These six sau-
sages are six cents for six.")

SPANISH

En un plato de trigo, comían tres tigres tristes trigo.[4]
("Three sad tigers ate wheat from a dish of wheat." *Tres
Tigres Tristes*, by the way, is the title of a novel by the
Cuban writer Guillermo Cabrera Infante.)
*Al obispo de Constantinople lo quieren desconstantinopoli-
zar.*[5] ("They want to deconstantinopleize the Bishop of
Constantinople.")

CATALAN

Setze jutges d'un jutjat
Mengen fetge d'un penjat.
El penjat es despenja i menja
Els fetges d'els setze jutges.[4]

("Sixteen judges of a court of law/Eat the liver of a hanged man./The hanged man unhangs himself and eats/The livers of the sixteen judges.")

ITALIAN

Appelle, figlio di Apollo, fece una palla di pelle di pollo.[5]
("Appelles, son of Apollo, made a ball of chicken skin.")
Chi troppo sale, cade di repente,
Precipitevolissimente.[5]
("He who rises too far falls suddenly,/Most precipitously.")

ROMANIAN

Romanian, at least by name, is the most romantic Romance language of them all. The donor of this Romanian tongue twister was forbidden to repeat it as a boy:

Popa poarta poala fetei.
Fata pupa poala popei.[6]

("The priest wears a girl's skirt./The girl kisses the priest's lap [i.e., cassock]." The definitions accompanying this submission included *pula,* "big prick," which presumably sounds much like *poala* when said fast.)

GERMAN

The German translation of "tongue twister" is *Zungenbrecher*—"tongue breaker." A few *Zungenbrechers:*
Wir weisen Weiber würden weisse, weiche Wasche waschen,
wenn wir wüssten wo warmes Wasser wäre.[7] ("We wise wives would wash white, soft wash, if we knew where there was warm water.")
Niemals ess' ich Essig; ess' ich Essig? Ich esse Essig nur mit

Gurken.[7] ("I never eat vinegar; do I eat vinegar? I eat vinegar only with cucumbers.")

Der Leutnant von Leuthen befahl seinen Leuten die Glocken von Leuthen nicht eher zu läuten, bis der Leutnant von Leuthen befahl seinen Leuten die Glocken von Leuthen zu läuten.[3] ("The lieutenant from Leuthen ordered his men not to ring the bells of Leuthen until the lieutenant from Leuthen ordered his men to ring the bells of Leuthen.")

SWEDISH

Packa Pappas kappsäck med fyra runda pepparkorn i en kopparpanna.[8] ("Pack Papa's knapsack with four round peppercorns in a copper pan.")

CZECH

Strč prst skrz krk.[9] ("Put your finger in your throat.")

HUNGARIAN

Az ipafái papnak fapipája van, tehát az ipafái papipipa papi fapipa.[3] ("The priest of Ipafa has a wooden pipe; that is, the priestly pipe of Ipafa, the priest's wooden pipe." The line is the refrain of an old Hungarian ditty.)

FINNISH

Pappilan apupapin papupata pankolla porisee.[10] (Allowing for a dearth of prepositions, the message here seems to be that "The pastor's helper in the pastor's home is boiling a pot of beans on an old-fashioned stove.")

JAPANESE

During my hunt for tongue twisters I was in correspondence about these and other word oddities with a

Japanese, self-described as "a miss or ms. in style, a flowering woman of age 28, a starving artist, say a poet and a translator, if i add." She forwarded several Japanese tongue twisters, which she called *hayakuchi kotoba*, "quick-mouth words." I'll unveil two of them in a moment; but first I must report her astonishing revelation that *Japanese men and women speak two entirely different languages.* Each sex understands the other's tongue, but uses only his or her own. The man says, *"Hara ga hetta"* for "I am hungry"; the woman, *"Onaka ga skimashita."* The man says, *"Meshi o kuo"* for "Let's have dinner"; the woman, *"Shokuji ni itashimasho."* The man says, *"Mizu o kurenaika?"* for "Will you give me some water?"; the woman, *"Omizu o kudasaimasenka?"*

The Japanese employ rigidly prescribed dialects—one, say, for a person of inferior status communicating with a superior; another for members of a specialized trade. The Imperial dialect is spoken only by the Royal Family, or by others when speaking to members of that family; to the majority of Japanese it is as mysterious as Greek, and far more esoteric than English. When Hirohito broadcast the Imperial rescript of surrender in 1945, it had to be glossed for the Japanese people.

But to have one language for men and a different language for women is even more remarkable, it seems to me. I wonder how Japanese feminists feel about that.

Writes my flowering Japanese ("miss or ms. in style"):

> there are two kinds of tongue-confusings.
> *category a.* she sells seashells at the seashore.
> *category b.* what kind of noise annoys an oyster?
> kids get a kick out of cat. b. because they lose the
> sense in this quick repeating process, they end up
> adding more meaningless "oy" sound somewhere
> and then they giggle up. i don't think cat. b. ever
> bothers any adults' tongues, there's no twist in my

tongue when I try cat. b. but cat. a. has a real authority to be called a tongue-biter, as in these *nama mugi, nana gome, nama tamago.*[11]

this simply means uncooked wheat (or barley or even oats: we don't have a one-word name for these crops); "fresh wheat, fresh rice, fresh egg." that's what it says, i'd never thought why it's so tongue-tangling up until this morning in this process of writing to you, i come to a very clear point of explanations. when we try to repeat this for 3 times at one breath we end up saying not *"nama mugi, nama gome, nama tamago,"* but *"naGa mugi, naGa gome, naGa tomago,"* or even *"naGa GuMi."* isn't it clear that the assimilation is happening, *m* assimilates with *g* and this *gumi* from *mugi* is metathesis, look, m*g* becomes g*m*. i'd like to hear you speak this if you go the same pattern we go.

tokyo-to-to tokkyo kyokakyoku.[11] this means the bonze (buddhist priest) painted or drew the picture of bonze on the folding screen skillfully, repeating this 3 times in a breath causes stammering or stuttering, i don't think there's a particular pattern for this but just easily get stuck in the middle of the stream.

it's famous or notorious that we japanese can't distinguish *l* and *r*. for me who try so hard to avoid the confusion this *l* and *r*, to name "charlotte rampling" (she's my favorite actress) is very tongue-biting. So i usually call her just "rampling." that's easier. this *r l r l* business is very tough even for me.

The more profoundly and humbly I ponder these *Zungenbrechers*, the greater grows their potential. What an innocent source of merriment the United Nations might become if the delegates vied only in tongue twisters instead of polemics! What a grand litmus paper tongue twisters would make in testing job applicants!

How crime would plummet if police officers could instantly determine the guilt or innocence of a suspect by fixing him with a gimlet eye, and ordering:
"Say now Shibboleth!"

CALCULUS
(Greek *khalix*, pebble)

A Calculus a Pebble was
  And still would be no more
Had count of fingers and of toes
  Not ended at a score

Which gave a mathematic rebel
  The thought of throwing in a Pebble.
Since endless pebbles line the sea
  We count now to Infinity.

A brainless pebble landed us
In Differential Calculus.

12
MY SERVANT
TRUTH

. . . in my neighborhood, it is unquestionably flat.

THE tea was steeping when old Betty Muxworthy, gone into churchyard these three hundred years, came rapping at the door. She has a tolerant fondness for me; I must be one of the few persons remaining who still recall with a leap of the heart Richard Blackmore's swashbuckling West Country romance *Lorna Doone,* for which Betty provided background commentary. It was she who ran the kitchen of giant, innocent Jan Ridd, who with mighty thews and simple heart won his impossibly fair and gentle Lorna from the wicked Doones, and laid their power waste. Betty had been supreme in her kitchen kingdom before the first Charles mislaid his head. She handily outlasted the Great Commoner who ruled but did not reign over England, and after him the second Charles, who reigned but did not rule, and the King James who followed.

Betty visits me, I suspect, principally for an opportunity to scold, which must be a great comfort to a woman who has lain three hundred years with her mouth stopped up, and no one to listen anyway.

She enjoys deriding me as a fraud, on the ground that I pretend to write books that others pretend to read. Betty believes there is no such thing as writing. She maintained to the very last that "people first learned things by heart, and then pretended to make them out from patterns done upon paper, for the sake of astonishing honest folk, just as do the conjurors."

"Men is desaving," she told me (as she used to tell Jan Ridd) over her third cup of tea; "but the most desaving of all is books, with their heads and tails, and speckots in 'em, like a peg as have taken the maisles. Some folks purtends to laugh and cry over them. God forgive them for liars!"

What use to tell her she was attacking the wrong target? Books, for all their heads and tails and speckots, do indeed form intelligible patterns. Few besides Betty will deny that a written language exists, and can be understood. But whether the language speaks truth is quite another matter. Sometimes we say what is convenient, and sometimes we lie for our own advantage; many a writer manipulates words to hoodwink readers, and many another to hoodwink himself. Truth is a Proteus who, seized by the throat, turns to a serpent and running water and a dragon and a wolf before he reveals what you accept as his actual shape; and even that final appearance may be a lie.

> I cried, "Truth, speak!" But Truth too buried lay
>   Inside my heart to raise its voice therefrom.
> I thrust the interfering heart away,
>   And cried, "Truth, speak!" Yet Truth continued mum.
> Abandoned heart, what truth has Truth to say?
>   . . . That Truth is dumb.

Two English boys were playing in their grandmother's room when one of them noticed that the old lady was reading her Bible. "Be quiet," he warned his brother; "Grandmother is swotting for her finals."

Mac has been gone from this coil for several years now, but when he visited me the other day he was as he had been the last time I saw him alive—swotting vigorously for his finals. Recurrent bouts of surgery had deprived him of an arm, a kidney, and a lung, all on his left side. His surviving members appeared poised to strike at any minute for improved working conditions. Yet there he sat serenely, giving his attention one-third to a cigarette, one-third to a martini on the rocks, and one-third to me.

"Truth, Willard," he said, "is subject to change on demand. According to the truth that you and I have been taught, there is no way in the world that we could be sitting here in your house on Fifty-first Street chatting—I dead and you, I have no doubt, lying in your study taking your afternoon nap. Yet here we are. And that is truth.

"I once believed," he went on, "that there was no life after death; but even before dying I realized I had been only half right. There is no Hell; but certainly there *is* a Heaven."

He was spelling out the truth about truth: that it is invaluable as a servant, but dreadful as a master. In circumstances matching those of Mac's last mortal months, the French lawyer in the verse below was equally ready to change his mind:

> A certain Paris *avocat*
> (An atheist, *bien entendu*)
> Revised his former point of view
> As he approached age *soixante-trois:*
> *"Je trouve," dit-il, "que plus en plus*
> *Je ne crois pas que je ne crois pas."*

To point out that the truths within our purview are changeable on demand, said Mac, is not to demean them. They are, after all, but splinters of that absolute truth which we assume to be changeless, but likewise unattainable:

> Herewith, a suggestion
> Your wits to enhance, sir:
> *The answer's the question;*
> *The question's the answer.*

All the better reason to retain control over humbler but more acceptable truths. Truth, in Mac's opinion, is Mac's opinion. As Shakespeare almost said, "There is nothing either true or false, but thinking makes it so."

I, for instance, look around for truths that bolster my ego:

> Ah! how melodious
> Are words that toady us!
> The rest—how odious!

Do not assume that either Mac's views or mine reflect terminal cases of solipsism. Though my opinion is the truth, if you bombard me with enough evidence I will change my opinion. The evidence will have to be overwhelming, to be sure, for I am a stubborn man. Nor will I accept logic as a substitute for objective evidence. Logic is as unreliable as reason:

> When I on reason reason, I
> In reason ask the reason why
> My reason passes reason by.
> Till reason reason satisfy,
> I reason reason is a lie.

In 1916, Charles Evans Hughes retired, on election night, aglow with a splendid truth: the voters had just chosen him President of the United States. As he slept, however, tardy returns from California reversed his victory. Reporters clamored for a statement from him. "The President cannot be disturbed," said an aide. Retorted one of the newsmen: "You go tell the President he is not the President."

Hughes had not been wrong; his truth was true until events overturned it. Nor was the editor of the *Chicago Tribune* wrong when on another election night, thirty-two years later, he ordered the banner headline:

DEWEY DEFEATS TRUMAN

The only trouble with his truth was that it was temporary. If that editor is still alive today, I do not think he still believes that Dewey defeated Truman; he doubtless changed his opinion when the evidence became overwhelming.

A scientist, or perhaps a philosopher, is said to have demonstrated that 2 + 2 does not necessarily come to 4. The once immutable thus becomes the merely fashionable, like women's clothes: long skirts today, miniskirts tomorrow, slacks the day after. Remember, when some new truth is announced, that it may be ephemeral. Education hailed as progressive today may be deemed regressive next week. Alligators, once protected as a threatened species, may multiply until they threaten the environment. Whooping cranes may reappear. The gentry may return to the inner cities. Radical students may become conservative. The growth in world population may decline, and the ocean prove unpollutable beyond the continental shelf.

Because my opinion is the truth, for as long as my opinion lasts, I prefer to withhold judgments on the new truths announced daily in the media. Do not believe too quickly. An untried truth may turn on you:

Pray, do not pat a horse with horns,
Lest he should tread upon your corns.

But if a newly revealed truth accords with your pre-conceptions and brings you pleasure, cleave to it. Make absolutes of your experiences. Did it rain ceaselessly the one weekend you were in Paris? Then let no one persuade you that Paris is not a city of relentless rain. Did a red-haired, stocky Swede pilfer your wallet? Be very wary, then, of red-haired, stocky Swedes.

Insist that the Almighty Himself put his cards face-up on the table before you accept his truths over yours:

> God argues constantly with me,
>   Till both of us are growing fed up.
> Says He to I, says I to He,
>   "Oh, *shed*dup, *shed*dup, *shed*dup, *shed*dup!"

When the evidence forces you to alter your opinion, do so gracefully:

> *VERITAS MUTATUR*
>
> Of truths I knew,
> Not one or two
> But quite a few
>   (In fact, a bunch)
> Have proved untrue.
> I have a hunch
> The truths I know
> Today may go
> That road also.
> Men mostly munch
> Roast crow for lunch.

When I was much younger, I wrote:

> I find it curiositive,
>   My good intentionals despite,
> That I am just as positive
>   When I am wrong as when I'm right.

186

By now, though, I know I am never in error. If you and I chance to disagree, I am the one with the straight of it. Like Huck Finn, I accept that the world taken as a whole may be round; but in my neighborhood it is unquestionably flat.

You may have been taken in by announcements of technological breakthroughs—steam power, radio, the phonograph, and so on. For you, these are truths. I assure you that in reality they are only mass delusions.

Well . . . I will make one partial exception. I grant a modicum of reality to the telephone. This is because when I used it in my childhood (we were on a forty-two-party line; our ring was a long, two shorts, and a long), I had to shout into the speaker to be heard. This accords with common sense. My belief in the telephone, however, does not go beyond local calls; a long-distance call flies in the face of nature.

But as I said before, I am open-minded to hard evidence. I concede that someone with a voice as powerful as that, say, of Enrico Caruso might be able to make himself heard over the long-distance telephone. I even concede that Noel Coward once did make himself so heard. I was surprised to learn this; it had never occurred to me that Coward had a particularly powerful voice until George Oppenheimer, the late screenwriter and drama critic, told me Coward once rang from London on the transatlantic telephone to condole with the actor Clifton Webb, in Hollywood, on the death of Webb's mother. Each time Coward sought to express his sympathy, Webb's roars of grief drowned him out. All the while the meter was ticking off pence, shillings, and pounds. Only after twenty costly minutes did Coward manage to override Webb's sobs by bellowing, "But *Clifton!* It's perfectly *normal* for a man to be an orphan at the age of seventy-three!"

George Oppenheimer, may his soul rest in peace, was an honorable man, so I accept that Noel Coward made himself heard over more than three thousand miles of Atlantic Ocean and another three thousand miles of North American continent. But the telephone was irrelevant. As an experienced actor, Coward knew how to make his voice carry.

If the telephone is a doubtful concept, electricity—as a force harnessed to furnish light and power—is ridiculous. Lightning, a manifestation of electricity, is real enough; doubtless it did strike Benjamin Franklin's kite; but the buck stops there. The increasing frequency of blackouts provides ample demonstration that even the most credulous human minds, when asked to carry an overload of impossibilities, will blow a fuse.

Flimflummery (run up, I suspect, by some advertising agency) disguises the reality that automobiles are really pulled by oxen, and railroad trains by Percherons. As for airplanes, they are chimeras; if you have been hoodwinked into believing humans can fly, just try to fly out the window.

The most absurd delusion of all is television. Hour after hour, day and night, millions of otherwise rational human beings sit hypnotized before an empty box. They have persuaded themselves that as they stare into it they see occurrences taking place hundreds or even thousands of miles away. They stare at a random whirl of electrons, and call it Johnny Carson.

Surely they know deep inside that there is no such thing as television. (There is no such person as Johnny Carson, either.)

If we fail to create our own truths, we are given the truths we deserve. The truth of an Irishman will never quite jibe with that of a Frenchman, nor the truth of a truck driver with that of a ballet dancer. Certain truths should remain provisional:

Last night you set my heart awhirl . . .
Unless it was some other girl.

Truth is what I see with my own eyes. No matter how
sternly my tape measure insists that line A and line B
below are exactly the same length, I know that line A is
shorter:

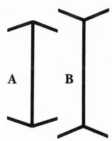

When I look at this cube, it shifts back and forth between two perspectives. Try it:

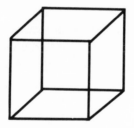

For me, either cube is the right one until it reverses
itself.

Truth is what my eyes see, and my ears hear, and my
mind accepts. No matter how true the words that enter
my right ear, they depart from the left with an entirely
different ring to them. Truth for me is the house on
Fifty-first Street. But none of this is the whole truth.
The whole truth is too terrible to gaze upon:

REFLECTION ON
FRESH FISH

As, from an idling launch, a seine
Trails back, so trails my net of brain;
And what it catches, great or small,
Is there entangled, once for all.
No human eye has seen the get
Proliferating in that net.

I count the floats that bob behind
To mark the meshes of my mind,
And know no winch shall ever turn
To heave that haul across the stern
And leave a Coelacanth of old
A-flap, expiring in my hold.

For in that web writhes such a spawn
As God would blench to gaze upon:
There Devilfish and Sea-hag squirm;
There Serpent coils with Erde-worm—
While there, by Mermaid's dimming eyes,
Old Triton drops his horn, and dies.

So I will cut my seine away,
And let it drift off down the bay,
And buy my fishes back on shore,
Refrigerated at the store.

I have mentioned that some of us arrive at new truths when swotting for our finals. All of us prefer to postpone those finals as long as possible. This is why sincere men and women (along with charlatans) are able to make millions of dollars by telling us how we can prolong for a few days or weeks peristalsis, heartbeat, respiration, and the like. Several of my friends hold as given truth that violent exercise is the best way to avoid heart attacks. The truth, in my opinion—and, I iterate, my opinion is the truth—is that a minimum of exercise is the best way to avoid heart attacks. My friends jog, make love hanging from chandeliers, and claim to play the curious game known as half-tennis, in which a solitary competitor serves, leaps the net, returns the serve, and continues until either he or himself has won game, set, and match. I relax in my hammock. I do not mean to asperse my friends; no doubt they are right according to their lights. Rather, they are right as long as they last. Most of them are gone now. I salute their memory in this verse:

JOGGER, JOG

Jogger, jog, and runner, run!
How I envy you your fun!
Agony distorts your face;
Yet I know some hidden grace—
Some ebullient, inner leaven—
Raises you to joggers' Heaven.

Jogger, gasping by the road,
Easing lungs of overload,
May I have your name, old scout?
If the leaven should run out—
If you jog off to your Maker—
I will call the undertaker.

JOCUS PARTITUS
= JEU PARTI = JEOPARDY

"Jocus partitus," *the Romans said:*
"The game's at even odds." This led,
When Frenchified, to jeu parti:
"The outcome's in uncertainty,"
And thence to "jeopardy" —for us,
"Exposure to siege perilous."
In jeopardy? The joke's on you,
For "joke" derives from jocus *too.*

13

A BRAYING
OF EASELS

$\underline{\underline{A}}$ESOP was into his fifth fable. "Old slave," I interrupted, "I did not invite you here to tell me fables. I have *read* your fables. What I want to know is, why did you make your points with animals instead of people?"

"Be patient, master," said Aesop; "bear in mind that this is the first chance I've had to tell a fable in twenty-five hundred years. Don't stop me if you've heard this: An Old Crab said to her son, 'Why do you walk sidewise like that, my son? You ought to walk straight.' The young Crab replied, 'Show me how, dear Mother, and I'll follow your example.' The Old Crab tried, but tried in vain, and then saw how foolish she had been to find fault with her son. The moral is—"

"I know: 'Example is better than precept.' But please answer my question. Since your fables aim at throwing light on human nature, why are nearly all of them about animals?"

"Because we think of animals as being simpleminded," said Aesop. "An animal can be used to sum up a single, uncomplicated point. My animals were clearly what they were, and said clearly what they had to say. The thoughts and activities of any human being are too complex for a quick summary. Yet the profounder the wisdom, the more simply it should be expressed. That is why—forgive my immodesty, master —Martin Luther cited my fables, more than two thousand years after my death, as 'wisdom literature,' second only to the Bible."

He was regarding me with one eye as he spoke; the other rolled loose in its socket. Aesop was an old man, and no beauty. If, as rumored, the Delphians flung him over a precipice because of his ugliness, it is hard to blame them. His bodily members appeared to be at war with one another. His left shoulder hunched up; his right hunched down. His torso was twisted, as if a giant had started to shape him into a corkscrew but stopped in the middle. His voice, however, was measured and compelling.

"I am hoping," I said, "that you will throw light on the way some words dealing with animals have become so integrated into the language that we have quite forgotten where they come from. Incidentally, it may interest you that one animal has scarcely changed its name in the two and a half millennia since you plunged to your death."

"What animal is that, master?"

"The cat. We have Old English *catt;* Old Norse *kottre;* Old Frisian and Middle Dutch *katte;* Dutch *kat;* Old High German *kazza;* German *Katze;* Old Norman, Anglo-Norman, and Middle English *cat;* French *chat;* Catalan *gat;* Spanish and Portuguese *gato;* Italian *gatto;* Irish and Gaelic *cat;* Welsh *cath;* Celtic *kattos;* Old Slavic *kotka;* Russian *kot,* tomcat; Lithuanian *kate;* Nubian *kadis;* and so on and on."

"To the early Romans, though, cat was *felis.*"

"Ah, but when the domestic cat was introduced into Rome in the Christian era, the Romans began saying *cattus.*"

"Let me tell you of an event," said Aesop—"not, I promise you, a fable—that occurred only a few years after my death, when the Persians and the Egyptians were at war. The Persian king, Cambyses, sent his cavalry into battle with the Egyptians carrying sacks of squalling cats, which they shook out among the enemy. This so demoralized the Egyptians, as cat worshipers, that they broke and ran; the battle made Persia master of Egypt for the next two hundred years. All because the Egyptians worshiped cats.

"But you wanted words," he went on, "where animal names are buried. Because men are riders of horses, they tend to describe as horses artifacts used for support—though the name of those andirons supporting the logs in your fireplace is from a Celtic word variously interpreted as 'heifer,' 'bull,' or 'goat,' and andirons are also called firedogs. A sawhorse supports logs for sawing; a cheval glass—horse glass, that is—supports a mirror mounted on swivels in a frame; an easel, from Dutch *ezel*, 'donkey,' is a standing frame holding a picture."

"Horses indicate rank, too," I said. "A 'man on horseback' is someone who seizes the reins of a country. Akin to Spanish *caballo*, 'horse,' and *caballero*, 'horseman,' are 'chivalry' and 'cavalier.' A footman, on the other hand, is a servant. From *pes*, Latin for foot, come 'pawn,' 'peon,' 'pedestrian.' "

"Also 'pioneer,' " said Aesop. "The first pioneer was simply a foot soldier—a fellow with large feet flattened by much tramping. A marshal was initially a horse servant, one who cared for horses; the word is from Old English *mearh*, horse, + *scealc*, servant. He was inferior to the constable—'count of the stable.' But the marshal went up in the world to become a person of substance, while a constable today is only a minor peace officer. Incidentally, while the word 'equestrian' comes from Latin *equus*, 'horse,' the word 'equerry,' though applied to an officer of nobles or princes charged with the care of their horses, does not; it is from French *écurie*, 'stable.' "

"You spoke of firedogs," I said. "Dogs are as intertwined in the language as horses. Not just in figures of speech—a dog's life, lucky as a dog, sick as a dog, that sort of thing—or descriptives like 'dogged persistence' and 'dog Latin'; but even in philosophy and astronomy."

"I assume your philosophic reference is to the Cynics of ancient Greece," said Aesop. "Their school styled itself *Kyōn,* 'dog,' because they foregathered at a gymnasium with a name of similar sound. Astronomically, you must have in mind the constellation of the hunter Orion; a star was supposed to be his dog and so was likewise called *Kyōn.* The Latins called the star *Caniculus,* 'small dog.' Since the arrival of Orion in the skies coincided with the hot, dry days of summer, it was also known, as we know it today, as *Sirius,* 'burning'; those hot days were the *dies caniculares,* 'dog days,' and they are dog days still."

I said, "The word 'baying' once referred to the barking of dogs in company; the expression 'at bay' referred to the hunted animal when, driven to extremity, he turns to face his barking pursuers."

" 'To set a dog on' was *harer* in Old French. It turned to *harasser* and, in English, to 'harass.' The canine origin is obliterated; 'harass' in English now means simply to vex or worry."

(Aesop, I reflected, must have been following language developments with some care in the twenty-five hundred years since he was thrown off that cliff. Well, he probably had little else to do.)

"In Middle English," he continued, "the track of an animal or person was a 'sleuth.' A dog trained to follow tracks was a sleuth hound, which in America became an epithet for 'detective,' the business of a detective being in part to follow tracks. But the last syllable sloughed away; the sleuth hound is now called the sleuth, as if the tracker were called the track.

"Not to wander off the sleuth—if you will permit the pun, master—in Old English, *lāst* also was a foot track. The word survives today in a cobbler's last. In Latin, the word for 'track' or 'furrow' was *lira; delirare* was 'to go off the track,' leading to the word 'delirium' for madness.

"To cultivate land, you have to rip a track in the soil. The French used for this purpose a triangular harrow once called a *herse.* A frame used for holding candles over the coffin of a person of distinction, being of similar shape, took the same name. From there it went on to mean, as it does in English 'hearse' today, 'a vehicle for carrying the bodies of the dead to the place of burial.' 'Rehearse' has the same source. When you rehearse your lines for a play, you are 're-harrowing.' "

"What about 'chevron,' " I asked, "from Latin *caper,* 'goat'? To caper is 'to skip like a goat.' Billygoats when fighting lock their horns together to form inverted V's. The shape led to the architectural term 'chevron' for two rafters locked together, and to the same term for the inverted V's of a sergeant's stripes."

"When you hear a bugle blow," said Aesop, "you don't think of an ox—yet a wild ox was once called bugle. Its horn was used as a drinking cup, and then as a musical instrument."

The talk turned to birds.

" 'Yokel,' " I suggested—"the green woodpecker; hence, woodpeckers being common in the country, a country fellow, a dolt."

"Pie," said Aesop. "The pie bird—called magpie because rustic lovers thought the birds chattered away like their own Mags—likes to make collections of miscellaneous objects; so when such oddments as fruit, meat, or cheese were thrown together and cooked in a pastry crust, the dish was called a pie. 'Chewet' was also an early word for a meat or fish pie, perhaps deriving from

French *chouette,* jackdaw or pie-bird, now an owl. That same pie-bird was called *haggess* in Scots and gave its name to the Scottish dish haggis, consisting mainly of the minced entrails of a sheep, boiled in the animal's maw."

"The Latins," I said, "called the woodpecker *picus*— whence *piccare,* 'to peck.' The Provençals added the meaning 'to jingle.' Since coins jingle, they called one of their small coins *picaioun,* which in nineteenth-century Louisiana became 'picayune.' The coin is gone, but the notion of its trifling value remains. So from the original Latin woodpecker we have a word unrelated in meaning: 'trifling.' "

"The Latins called a bird's beak a *rostrum,*" said Aesop. "They extended its meaning to the beak or prow of a ship. In 338 B.C. the Romans decorated the orators' platform in the Roman forum with the beaks of ships captured from Antium, and named the platform for the beaks—*rostrum.* Today a rostrum is any platform for public speaking."

"Then there is 'gorge,' " I said, "as in 'His deceitfulness makes my gorge rise.' In the fifteenth century, the crop, or internal sac where a bird's food first is held after swallowing, was called 'gorge.' A hundred years later 'gorge' came to mean the contents of the human stomach."

"A bird's crop," said Aesop, "is frequently filled with worms. It is a point to be remembered the next time you eat vermicelli—'little worms' in Italian."

"*Geranion* in Greek," I said, "meant 'little crane.' Geraniums take their name from the fact that many have thin, tapering fruits reminiscent of the beak of a crane. Nasturtiums are named, for their pungent smell, after Latin *nasus,* 'nose,' + *turtium,* a form of *torquere,* 'twist' —'nose twister.' "

" '*Torquere*' is the root of 'tortoise,' too," said Aesop,

"after the beast's crooked feet; also of 'torture,' which frequently involves the twisting of bodily members; and, in law, of 'tort'—something crooked, bent.

"You mentioned geraniums and nasturtiums. I have created fables about plants as well as animals. A Fir-tree was boasting to a Bramble—no, don't stop me, master —and said, somewhat contemptuously, 'You poor creature, you are of no use whatever. Now, look at me: I am useful for all sorts of things, particularly when men build houses; they can't do without me then.' But the Bramble replied, 'Ah, that's all very well; but you wait till they come with axes and saws to cut you down, and then you'll wish you were a Bramble and not a Fir.' The moral is, 'Better poverty without a care than wealth with its many obligations.'

"Further to plants," he went on, "the stamen, the male organ of a flower, meant in Latin the warp in a loom— the series of vertical threads crossed by the woof. This meaning narrowed to 'thread,' in appearance like a stamen.

"Metaphorically, however, *stamen* hustled off in another direction, following the lead of its plural, *stamina*. Inasmuch as the three Fates spun the threads of life, *stamina* were as integral to human existence as threads to a cloth; life's character and durability were determined by the threads that composed it. In English, 'stamina' became a singular noun connoting 'endurance, staying power.' A considerable reach from a thread, or even the male organ of a plant.

"And I give you the fragrant yellow jonquil. It is named from Latin *juncus,* a marsh plant, 'rush.' Stems of *juncus* were woven into mats and baskets; the latter were used specifically to hold a kind of sweetened, curdled milk, soon named 'junket' after its container. In William Adlington's sixteenth-century translation of *The Golden Ass,* delicacies listed included 'bread pastries, tartes, custardes, and other *ionkettes* dipped in honey.' A junket next became a 'feast or banquet.' Nowadays it is a different kind of feast: 'a trip taken by a public official at public expense.' "

"The Anglo-Saxons," I said, "used *wealh* or *wealisc* to denominate Celtic or Roman foreigners. From *wealh* and *wealisc* derived both 'Welshmen'—the Celts driven back into what is now Wales—and 'walnuts,' first *wealh*-nuts, 'foreign' nuts. The same root is in 'Walloon,' applied by the French to the conquered Celts and southern Belgians."

"Back to animals, master," said Aesop. "The word 'fur'—Old French *fuerre*—at one time meant simply the casing of a dagger or sword. From that it became the lining of a garment. The English too would 'fur' a cloak with cotton, wool, or eiderdown. But because the most luxurious linings were the pelts of certain beasts—weasel, badger, ermine—the usage became restricted to linings obtained from such animals. 'Fur' now stands for a pelt even when the animal is still running around in it."

"Consider the ramifications of 'cow,' " I said. "Latin *vacca* for 'cow' led to Spanish *vaquero*, one who attends cows. 'Buckaroo' hobson-jobsoned *vaquero* into English. When it turned out that inoculation with a substance engendered by cowpox prevented smallpox in humans, we named the substance 'vaccine' after that long-dead Latin cow."

"A cow's milk in Greek was *gala*," said Aesop. "Because of their milky appearance, we refer to the 'galaxies' in the sky, and call our own the Milky Way. Did you realize, by the way, that the heavenly galaxies and the humble garden lettuce have the same word root? 'Lettuce' comes from Latin *lac*, milk, because some varieties exude a milky juice.

"Both 'cattle' and 'capital' derive from Latin *capitalis*, relating to the head, or chief; a man's wealth was once measured by the number of cattle he owned. Three words for cattle—Latin *pecu,* Old French *fé,* and Old English *feoh*—took on the meaning of 'property.' *Pecu* led to 'pecuniary,' 'impecunious,' 'peculate'—and also to 'peculiar,' one's property being *peculiar* to oneself. *Fe* and *feogh* joined hands to mean 'fee,' a payment for services."

"A bulldog," I said, "though once used for bullbaiting, is named not for "bull" but for French *boule,* 'ball,' from the roundness of its head. And the 'pole' in 'polecat' is from Middle French *pol,* the male of the chicken. A polecat was 'a cat-like beast that kills chickens.' "

"Cats remind me of mice," said Aesop. "In Latin, a 'little mouse' was a *musculus*—the original of 'muscle.' The Romans applied the name to the great muscles of the arm and leg, thinking they looked like mice, with the tendons serving as the tails. They similarly fancied that the swollen veins surrounding a tumor resemble the legs of a crab sticking out from its shell; 'cancer,' as all astrology buffs know, is Latin for 'crab.' "

" 'Urchin,' " I said, "from Latin *ericius,* was formerly the common English name for a hedgehog. The sea urchin is so-called because, like a hedgehog, it is prickly. In the sixteenth century, people began applying the epithet 'urchin' to ragged, rough-haired street children. We now use it affectionately for children in general."

"Speaking of sea creatures," said Aesop, "in Middle English a flatfish was a *butte.* When eaten on holy days, it was called a 'haly'—holy—butte. Hence 'halibut.' "

I nodded, and he went on:

"We have not mentioned insects. The Italians used to describe the arrow of a crossbow as a *moschetto,* 'little fly.' The French borrowed the word as *mousquet* for early gunpowder-fired hand weapons, which in English became 'muskets.' But English also reserved the Spanish name for 'little fly,' *mosquito,* to mean a particularly annoying biting insect. The Greeks named it *kōnōps,* and called a netting hung for protection against it a *kōnōpion.* The English referred to the netting as a 'canopy,' and the French to the couch so protected as a *canapé.* When they invented a dish consisting of a piece of bread and a savory they thought it resembled a *canapé,* and gave it the same name. A canapé has come a long way from a mosquito netting."

"The larva of an insect," I said, "is from Latin *larva,* ghost—"

"Ah yes. Linnaeus, father of classification, used the word in the sense of 'mask,' on the ground that the imago, or grown insect, cannot be identified by comparison with its larval state."

"Carry this note on the subject away with you," I said:

> From unlikely looking *larva*
> Nature cleverly doth carve a
> Grown *imago:* Cockahoopa,
> *Larva* turns itself to *pupa*—
> And from *pupa* doth one day go
> Flying off, a grown *imago.*

"A verse of the less memorable sort," said Aesop. "It makes me think of the Gnat that alighted on one of the horns of a Bull, and remained there for a considerable time. When it had rested sufficiently and was about to fly away, it said to the Bull, 'Do you mind if I go?' The Bull merely raised his eyes and remarked, without interest, 'It's all one to me; I didn't notice when you came, and I shan't know when you go away.'

"The moral is, master," he added, fixing me with his right eye while his left rotated, "that flies, like writers, may be of more consequence in their own eyes than in the eyes of their neighbors."

On that note, which I could not construe as a compliment, he departed. I am still trying to draw an overall moral from our conversation. Perhaps it is that a good bit of the beast remains in all of us, even in our language.

DISASTER AND SHLIMAZL

Disaster. A calamity. (Latin *dis* + *astro*, ill-starred)
Shlimazl. An unlucky man. (Yiddish, from Middle High German *slimp* + Hebrew *mazal*, ill-planeted)

The man ill-starred is doomed, ere dead,
  To meet disaster;
But ah! the man ill-planeted
  Will meet it faster.

Malignant stars long bided time
Ere they at last got off the dime
  On Lear to swoop.
Now, a shlimazl is a chap
Who INSTANTLY *into his lap*
  Receives the soup.

14

THE PEACOCKS

. . . they lay squozen,
Tugging—half-asleep, half-frozen.

MY equity in the house on Fifty-first Street is an inner matter, not subject to transfer of title. Though the point is academic, it has occurred to me that a property which by a shift of thought can be transmuted into an object of choice—a farm, a city, or, indeed, a universe —would fetch a staggering sum on the real estate market. Nor do I see how these advantages could be taxed.

Only the other day, for example, I converted the house on whim into a mansion overlooking the Atlantic —an instantaneous process less exasperating than driving a hundred miles from New York City to East Hampton in boiling weather and bumper-to-bumper traffic. I had a weighty project in train—an essay on the relationship between correct pronunciation and clear writing— and it seemed a pleasant idea to work on the veranda, where I could raise my head occasionally to look past a sloping lawn and over a privet hedge to a deserted beach, a gentleness of surf, and blue water beyond.

But it was a warm, lazy day—my own fault, for I had ordered it that way—and my wicker chair had a comfortably padded bottom. My thoughts must have wandered as I wrote, for my treatise came out like this:

> The (.), which marks the end
> Of any thought that one has penned,
> Will have no chance my thoughts to rout,
> For I propose to leave it out

The (,), though, I have not banned;
It's there to help me understand:
"The day before I rode a llama"
Requires for sense a middle (,)

(" "), at my command,
Enclose a phrase that's secondhand;
My wittiest creative sparks
Should really wear (" ")

The (:)'s tricky: don't confuse
Its peristalsis with its muse:
The verbal sort anticipates;
The other kind evacuates

When there remains no breath of life in
A (;), (—), or (=),
With ostentation funerarial
Provide them a respectful burial,

Clad obitally in Hic Jacets
And neatly tucked away in ([ ])

That was not at all what I had intended to write, but
I was not bothered. A man cannot be serious all the
time, I told myself. Why should I worry about punctuation now, with a pampering sun and a fluffy breeze
alternately caressing my face? Let work go hang. I
picked up the anthology of light verse that lay in readiness beside my typewriter and began thumbing through
it, looking for lines that might make me smile.

I lifted my eyes from the page—or had I been dozing?—just in time to see a peacock emerge from the
hedge at the foot of the lawn. He was engaged in an

odd business: by touches of his beak, now on one side, now on the other, he was maneuvering before him a shining bubblelike globe, so light that it bobbed. It was the size of the spun-glass balls that float during the Christmas season on the tree at Rockefeller Plaza.

Other peacocks followed the first, each trundling its own globe. Though there was no appearance of purpose, they edged these along until eventually the whole glittering lot lay like a cluster of Easter eggs in a dip in the lawn. Their task accomplished, the peacocks appeared to dismiss their charges from their minds; they scratched aimlessly about, and finally wandered back one after another through the hedge.

I was aware that I had witnessed a heavenly metaphor. The verses had separated from the book in my lap to become bobbing, glittering bubbles, and their authors iridescent fowl. Masters of light verse—of the playful, the comic, the nonsensical, and the absurd— had left the pages to glitter in the afternoon sunlight. I thought I could even identify a few: Dorothy Parker,* who nipped any peacock that got in her way; F.P.A., with the long, ridiculous beak; and Ogden Nash, who occasionally concealed his head under his wing, as if wondering what he was doing in such exotic company.†

I watched all afternoon long; but the peacocks did not return.

* I was well aware that Dorothy Parker was a peahen. But she looked like a peacock.

† There were many more: Keith Preston; T. A. Daly; G. K. Chesterton; Wallace Irwin; Charles Edward Carryl; A. O. Herbert; Samuel Hoffenstein; Arthur Guiterman; Morris Bishop; Don Marquis; Walter de la Mare; Owen Wister; Christopher Morley; Hilaire Belloc; Oliver Herford; Edmund Clerihew Bentley; Bert Leston Taylor; J. C. Squire; Carolyn Wells; Gelett Burgess; Noel Coward; Oliver St. John Gogarty; Arthur Quiller-Couch; T. R. Ybarra; Newman Levy; Corey Ford; Frank Sullivan; Louis Untermeyer. A few still live behind the hedge—and long may they thole. No tombstones yet lean over John Betjeman, E. B. White, Melville Cane, J. B. Morton, or David McCord. But they roll few spun-glass balls nowadays.

My contentment turned to depression then. I began to wonder whether I had not been witness to the vanishing of a lovely art—the art of creating witty, sometimes nonsensical poetry. It seemed to me for a while that I could not rediscover even in the kingdom of my own brain the laughter that comes when in obedience to a concealed discipline Judy beats Punch with the inflated bladder of a calf, and Nonsense chases them both about a children's stage.

Where, I wondered, had the peacocks gone?

I had heard it remarked, with a wise nodding of heads, that the world has become an extremely busy place, full of worries and preoccupations, and that busy people have no time to waste on crafting—or, for that matter, sorting out—the kind of poetry in which the language is part of the joke, as a raisin is part of a mince pie. Our times are too abustle for such quirkish elegance as

> Much ado there was, God wot;
> He would love, and she would not

or even such an atrocity as William McGonagall's

> The Hen it is a noble beast;
>   The cow is more forlorner,
> Standing in the rain
>   With a leg at every corner.

Surely McGonagall, the worst poet in the world, was no peacock. But he was funny.

A plague, I had been told, is burrowing into our culture; its buboes are swelling in our loins. Our sensible projects for improving the world gain no more ground than a squirrel running its head off in a cage; the Devil smacks his lips at the flavor of our best intentions; life insists on its imperfections. Why these truisms hit us so unexpectedly and demoralized us so deeply may be a puzzlement; but they did. Verse for verbal pleasure, whether rough-grained or fine-boned, was declared to have no antibodies for such a sickness. The temper of the times called for the kind of humor that followed the breakdown of the Three Mile Island nuclear plant, when newspapers amused their readers with such weather forecasts as "Sunny; temperature 3,000 degrees," and "Showers this afternoon; survival probability 45 percent." By comparison with wit that has the skull showing through, playful verse seems pretty tame, if not downright antisocial. If you are oppressed night and day by the fear that the very survival of humankind is in jeopardy, your misery is likely to prefer the company of such macabre humor as this quatrain of Paul Dehn's:

> O nuclear wind, when wilt thou blow
> That the small rain down can rain;
> Christ, that my love were in my arms
> And I had my arms again.

You may even consider your appreciation of such gallows graffiti a mark of moral superiority. If you see yourself in a Laingian world where sanity is madness and madness sanity—if, that is, you have lost your sense of sense—you can scarcely be expected to feel warmly toward the opposite side of the coin of sense, which is nonsense. You will find it more comfortable to rub your hands over other sorts of coin—the Poem of Self-Expression, for instance, in which lumpishness outweighs deftness and vacuity is misnamed profundity—than to join the challenge of playfulness to the dismal and the dark. One such challenge is light verse, which has to be either very, very good or nothing; it must stand or fall not simply by its intentions, but by its subtlety, precision, intellectual discipline, and ability to disarm.

Perhaps I am overly doleful. Times may be changing. Light verse is again beginning to appear in such newspaper columns as "Metropolitan Diary" (*The New York Times*), and even in correspondence from my own readers. Perhaps the buboes have begun to shrink. Perhaps the plague is beginning to subside.

Hurriedly, that golden afternoon, as if I were running out of time, I wrote the verses that follow. They are no peacock eggs. Yet they may lead you to reflect, "Well, at least I can do no worse than he does." So you may find yourself constructing playful verse of your own; and someone else may follow your example; and a summer afternoon may arrive when once again we see, looking down the lawn, an ostentation of peacocks, glittering as they scratch in the grass around a nest of shining eggs.

There is no etymological connection between "unkept" (from "keep"—as "an unkept woman") and "unkempt" (from *kemb*, "to comb," as a woman who is unkept because she is unkempt):

> A man in my town, Cal y-clempt
> (Who claimed at love to be adempt),
> Of winning Winnie's favors dreamt.
> Tiptoe to Winnie's bed Cal crempt,
> And quick to Winnie's side he leampt
> To launch his amorous attempt.
> Alas! Cal's corpus was unkempt,
> And Cal's inducements were inempt;
> So though he begged and raged and wempt,
> She turned her back on him and slempt.

My next verse was a sex-soaked clerihew:

DON JUAN AT COLLEGE

Don Juan
Carried on
Till they switched him from Biology
To Abnormal Psychology.

Only a bit less absorbing than sex, I reflected as I gazed from my veranda down the sunlit lawn, is grammar. Consider, for instance, the defining phrases (or clauses) called restrictive and nonrestrictive. The restrictive phrase, being essential to the meaning of the statement it occurs in, is not set off by punctuation from the noun it qualifies. In "The story you have heard is true," "you have heard" is a restrictive phrase. But if the meaning is only that you have *heard* the story is true, the phrase becomes nonrestrictive, and *is* set off by commas: "The story, you have heard, is true." The verse below does not attempt to clarify these distinctions; it simply puts them in a gastric setting.

I grant you, the Restrictive Phrase
Tastes fine if spread with mayonnaise
And sprinkled with cayenne.
Remember, though, that having dined,
If you feel ill and change your mind,
It won't come up again.

The Unrestrictive Phrase, however,
Barfs up if tickled by a fevver,
As fishlets leave their mammas.
So if you're queasy when you swallow,
This rule of grammar always follow:
Enclose your bite in commas.

A friend named Pamela is the inspiration for this verse:

BACTRIAN CAMELS
HAVE TWO HUMPS

I met on a tram in exotic Siam
  (Known as *tramela* there in Siamela)
Three Campbellite camels—a sire, dam, and lamb
  (In Siamese, *Camela famila*).

The sire was Ben-Amelek Ben-Abraham,
  A curious name for a Bactrian *cam*
  (Abbreved Siamese for a *camela*).
Ma'am Ben-Abraham was a well-trodden dam
  (Whom tram-trippers taunted as Bactrius Mam
  On account of her uberous *mammala*)
Who suckled a Campbellite camel named Pam,
  A truncated version of Pamela.

And what has becam of that *Camela* fam
Since they traveled away on their Siamese tram
I've never been told, and I don't give a damn,
  Or even a Siamese *dammela*.

The shadows were lengthening. But why should I hurry away, I asked myself, when here in the mansion by the sea, as in the house on Fifty-first Street, I had power to stop the sun itself? So stop the sun and time I did, to scribble these two last verses by way of farewell to my peacocks:

I WOULD I WERE FLUENT IN LATIN

I would I were fluent in Latin
  Instead of deplorably weak;

I would that my schooling were pat in
  Rhetoric, Hebrew, and Greek.

How greatly 'twould help me to win you
  If classical praise I could spin
In words of Herculean sinew
  And hints of Lilithean sin!

With apocopes I would pursue you;
  With tmesis and zeugma I'd seek;
But alas, dear, I only can woo you,
  In absence of Latin and Greek,
    With one rude toast:
    "You're the most!"

ROYAL OTTOS I AND II

(Otto I and Otto II, his son, were joint emperors of Germany
from A.D. 961 to 973.)

Royal Ottos I and II
  Shared a single bed.
("Single" here will hardly do;
The bed had room for quite a few.
I shall call it, *entre nous,*
  "Expansible," instead.)
Royal Ottos I and II
  Shared a single queen.
("Single" doesn't sound quite right;
  I shall call her "bipartite.")
The Ottos shared the bed all night,
  And she shared in between.

Royal Ottos I and II
  Shared a single blanket.
("Single" here is poorly chosen;

Let's say "narrow"; they lay squozen,
Tugging—half-asleep, half-frozen,
  Each the blanket yankit.)

Royal Ottos I and II
  Shared a single crown.
("Single," yes; the great crown sped
Back and forth from head to head
All day, and all night too in bed
  Beneath the eiderdown.)

APPENDIX:
The Peacocks

William Cole, a prolific anthologist of light verse and no
mean craftsman in the form himself, says he can suggest no
promising young writers in the field, "for they have no out-
let." He excepts John Updike, for whom comic poems are a
sideline. A partial list of serious poets who write frivolity on
occasion includes John Hollander, Anthony Hecht, George
Starbuck, X. J. Kennedy, Howard Moss, William Jay Smith,
and Edward Field. Mr. Cole's chronological ranking of the
greatest masters of light verse:

- Thomas Hood, 1799–1845
- Charles Stuart Calverley, 1831–1884
- Lewis Carroll, 1832–1898
- W. S. Gilbert, 1836–1911
- Hilaire Belloc, 1870–1953
- Ogden Nash, 1902–1971

"I feel bad about leaving out Arthur Guiterman and Morris
Bishop and Samuel Hoffenstein," says Mr. Cole, "but there it
is."

SILLY, FOND

"Silly" first meant luck and happiness; then deserving of pity; then feebleminded. "Fond" meant first foolish, silly; then foolishly affectionate; then simply affectionate.

What is silly? *What is* fond?
Silly *once was luck.*
Fond *was* silly, *and the bond*
Between the two has stuck.
You are like a drop of dew;
You are like a lily.
I am very fond *of you;*
This is very silly.

15

A SLAVE TO
FASHION

I FEEL no bitterness at never having been listed among the ten best-dressed men of the year. Disappointment, yes; regret, yes, at the flawed standards reflected in such mistaken judgments; but certainly no bitterness. Yet I must admit that when I found Beau Brummell making himself at home in the house on Fifty-first Street and I contrasted my apparel with his, I found myself defensive, even a little edgy.

He was wearing a dark blue coat, with a white waistcoat and sage-green breeches that fitted his legs like a natural skin. His cravat was a large square of cerulean muslin, wrapped around his neck and knotted in front. The living-room floor was heaped with discarded cravats—squares of muslin, lawn, or silk, folded cornerwise into an elaborate band. "What are those, Beau?" I asked.

"Sir," he said, lightly caressing the cravat at his neck, "those are my failures." (There was an air of hauteur about him; yet it probably meant only that the collar of his shirt projected over his cheeks, making it difficult for him to alter the position of his head.)

"Failures?" I asked, puzzled.

"Yes; they are the cravats I tried and set aside when dressing this morning."

"Do you mean to say that you still spend as much time on your clothes as you did when you were alive?"

"Oh, more; in my latter days, as you know, I fell on

hard times, and became quite slovenly; I am making up for that now. Besides, I have found a most agreeable position where I am staying, and it requires that I be well dressed."

"What position is that?"

"I am a clothing salesman."

"Wait a minute," I said. "Did one of my interfering friends send you here? I am not in the market. I am perfectly satisfied with the clothes I am wearing right now."

"No doubt," he said, gazing with disapproval on my baggy tweeds. "In any event, that is not why I have come. You are said to take an interest in word origins; I would like to tell you the origins of some words connected with clothing and personal appearance."

"I already know a few," I said. "But go ahead."

"Take 'grisette,' for instance. It is an inferior gray fabric, which at one time was the only cloth poor Frenchwomen could afford for their dresses. They wore it so constantly that the name of the cloth became that of the wearer. For generations, Frenchwomen of the lowest economic stratum have been known as grisettes."

"The English have a cheap gray fabric," I said, "called 'hodden.' "

"Actually, hodden doesn't have to be gray. It is simply coarse woolen cloth. We think of it as gray because in 1724, for the sake of a rhyme in his poem 'Gentle Shepherd,' Ramsay reversed the words 'gray hodden,' writing them 'hodden gray.' Later writers copied and hyphenated the words, until the public came to think of 'hodden' as a shade of gray."

"Did men wear seersucker suits in your day?" I asked.

"I do not believe the fabric had been imported yet. But the word for the thin striped crimped fabric corrupts a Persian expression meaning 'milk and sugar'—

shir-o-shakhar: 'seersucker.' Which reminds me of your word 'gabardine,' describing a twilled fabric. It is named after 'gaberdine,' a loose upper garment, which in turn derives its name from a Middle High German word for 'pilgrimage.' I suppose pilgrims wore gaberdines when they set off for the Holy Land."

"Some Orthodox Jews still wear gaberdines," I said.

"Then," he proceeded, "there is 'cassock.' It is from Turkish *quzzaq,* meaning 'nomad, adventurer, light horseman.' These types often wore long cloaks, and the cloak came to be called *quzzaq,* anglicized as 'cassock.' It is now applied commonly to ecclesiastical tunics. The Cossacks, or Kazakhs, a people of Turkish origin in the Union of Soviet Socialist Republics, once famous as the light horsemen of the Russian army, were given the name because their customary garb was a *quzzaq.*"

I felt a twinge of irritation at the contrast between my rumpled apparel and Beau Brummell's finery. "I have seen you referred to as 'dapper,'" I said slyly. "It's a disagreeable word, don't you think? It reminds me of Agatha Christie's detective Hercule Poirot, who was always so fastidiously dressed, or of some undergrown fellow with a hairline moustache and spats."

"I do not know your Hercule Poirot, but 'dapper' did not first mean fussy about appearance. It meant 'stout, heavy.' Old Prussian had a related word meaning 'large,' and Russian has one meaning 'plump.' 'Stout,' by the way, was considered a flattering epithet once. It descended from an Old High German word for proud, fierce, brave. It had no connotation of corpulence until the nineteenth century."

"So a dapper man was a stout man, and a stout man was a brave man—'stout fellow,' we still say. Incidentally, would you call *me* dapper?"

"I would not," said Beau Brummell. "But on the other hand, neither are you pilgarik."

"What is 'pilgarik'?"

"The word developed from a mispronunciation of 'peeled garlic.' It means 'bald.' You are not bald. You are, however, puny."

"I am *not* puny," I said sharply.

"Do not take offense. 'Puny' is not a pejorative word. It is from French *puisné*, 'born afterward,' and so, naturally, smaller. 'Puisne,' pronounced 'puny,' is still used in law; a puisne judge is a junior judge. The eight Associate Justices of the United States Supreme Court, despite their eminence, are all puisne judges. Oh—let me tell you about the origin of 'frump.' "

I do not know why, but I was beginning to take his remarks personally. "I am *not* a frump," I said.

"I did not say you were. The description is generally reserved for a dowdy woman. I simply thought it might interest you that 'frump' is from a dialect word meaning 'wrinkle.' "

"I cannot deny," I said, "that my face is increasingly frumpish. Nor, incidentally, can I call myself a man of mighty thews. Some time back, my physician reported me in good shape, except that I had few abdominal muscles left. On his next examination he said I was still in good shape, except that I had *no* abdominal muscles left. No thews."

"Before Shakespeare's time, any good quality or virtue was referred to as a thew," said Brummell. "The bard broadened the meaning to include bodily powers, and Scott developed the present association with sinews and tendons."

"In that original sense of virtue, I *am* a man of mighty thews."

"By the way," said Beau Brummell, "have you ever had pinkeye?"

I said, "You are becoming ridiculous. Yes, I suppose I had pinkeye in my childhood. Why?"

"Why do you think the disease is called pinkeye?"

"Because the eye is inflamed, and so pink."

"Quite wrong. 'Pink' is from Dutch *pinck*, 'small' (which is why your little finger is your 'pinky'), plus *oog*, eye. Your eyelids were inflamed; your eyes were half-closed, and so small. The color pink had nothing to do with it."

"I do not have pinkeye," I said.

He pounced. "Of course not," he said, whipping an order book from his coat pocket. "But if I may say so, your clothes are a disgrace. May I show you some swatches for a suit?"

I rid myself of Beau Brummell soon after that. No gentleman who is supposed to be discussing the connection between words and clothes would switch the subject to pinkeye in order to close a sale.

CHAGRIN

Mental disquietude or distress. (From Turkish *saghri,* rump
of a horse, whence shagreen, a leather of granulated
appearance, is prepared. —Weekley's *Etymological Dictionary.*)

Should Turkish horse dare misdemean,
The rider wallops its shagreen—
That is to say, he lands a thump
Upon the fractious horse's rump;
From which vexation of the skin
Derives our English word chagrin.

And when the rump is thumped enough,
The skin thereof grows very tough;
And when at length the horse is dead,
That tough shagreen's *to leather made.*
Chagrin, shagreen—*they're both, my dear,*
The product of a horse's rear.

16

THE ZIGGURAT
OF BABEL

IT was F.D.R., all right, with a lap robe thrown over his knees, and his chin upthrust, and his cigarette holder upthrust from his lips. I asked him to what I owed the honor of his visit.

"It is a matter of some urgency, Willard. I have had leisure these past few years to observe my fellow Americans at their work and play. And I have concluded that something is wrong. A major change is needed."

"A revival of morals, perhaps?" I said. "More Moral Majority? That sort of thing?"

"No, the problem is far too serious for such half measures. The country needs a New Deal."

"But we've *had* a New Deal, Mr. President. Don't you remember? You gave it to us yourself. Well, perhaps not *gave* it—the cost was quite high—but at least *started* it."

" 'New Deal' may not be the best slogan for what I have in mind this time. I am proposing a constitutional amendment to prohibit jargon."

"Mr. President!" I exclaimed, aghast. "You of all people know what happened when we tried to prohibit drinking. Prohibition doesn't work. You were the man who did most to cancel the whole idea."

"But jargon is a far more pernicious menace to mankind than alcohol ever was. We *have* to make this new Prohibition work. The reason I ran for a fourth term in World War II was not to see the war through—victory

237

was already assured—but because I intended, once peace was established, to cap my Presidency by abolishing jargon. It became my principal goal the day I received a blackout directive that went this way:"

> Such preparations shall be made as will completely obscure all federal buildings occupied by the federal government during a raid for any period of time from visibility by reason of internal or external illumination. Such obscuration may be obtained either by blackout construction or by terminating illumination.

"Jargon, to be sure," I agreed. "How did you handle it?"

"I scratched it out, and wrote instead, 'Cover the windows, and turn out the lights.' "

"Admirable!" I said. "You are the very man, if I may say so, to appreciate an outstanding example of jargon from my files. It is a takeoff by the late Ivor Brown on the Lord's Prayer."

President Roosevelt blew a smoke ring. "I came here," he said, "to fight jargon, not listen to it. And I need your help."

"Do me this one favor first: You recite the Lord's Prayer, and after each verse I will give Mr. Brown's version."

He agreed with some reluctance—I told myself he must want my help badly indeed—and we alternated:

Roosevelt	Espy
Our Father, who art in heaven,	Oh Parent, at present deemed to be domiciled in the stratosphere

ROOSEVELT	ESPY
Hallowed be thy Name.	May Your name (to be entered in triplicate in block letters) be established and maintained on the highest level of sacrosanctity
Thy kingdom come,	May you be allotted and obtain an area of control with appropriate powers of administration
Thy will be done, On earth as it is in heaven.	May Your policy be fully executed on a geo-political basis as well as in the normal stratospherical sphere of influence
Give us this day our daily bread.	We should be obliged for Your attention in providing for our nutritional needs and for so organizing distribution that our daily intake of cereal filler be not in short supply.

Here I interpolated: "James B. Minor put that plea for daily bread like this:"

> We respectively petition, request, and entreat that due and adequate provision be made, this day and the date hereinafter subscribed, for the satisfying of these petitioners' nutritional requirements and for the organizing of such methods of allocation and distribution as may

be deemed necessary and proper to assure the reception by and for said petitioners of such quantities of baked cereal products as shall, in the judgment of the aforesaid petitioners, constitute a sufficient supply thereof.

F.D.R. was shuddering, perhaps from shock, as he recited his next line:

And forgive us our trespasses,

Further we should be grateful if all sentences recorded against us for misdemeanors and malfeasances be kept under constant review with the possibility of subsequent cancellation.

As we forgive those who trespass against us.

It would be fair to remember that we are adopting an analogous policy with regard to those who have inflicted injury upon ourselves.

And lead us not into temptation,

Avert from us all redundant opportunities for delinquency and ethical deviation

But deliver us from evil . . .

And initiate protective measures to safeguard us from any antisocial activities or tendencies to recidivism

"Enough!" said F.D.R. "I will condone this sacrilege no longer." And he flatly refused to continue reciting. So I served him a Scotch and soda and myself a Scotch on the rocks, and he returned to business.

"Willard," he said, "you are not a busy man, and you are supposed to have a sentimental concern for words. In addition you have a background in public relations, though I gather not a scintillant one. I am therefore asking you to lead a movement. I want you to make jargon as abhorrent to every American as matricide."

"Mr. President," I said, "I sympathize with you. But I must refuse."

"*Refuse?*" He stared. "How can you, a patriotic American, refuse to help your country in its hour of desperate need?"

"Because God," I said, "is on the other side."

And I told him the story.

No one was visible in the easy chair opposite my desk. I might not even have noticed the slight indentation of the cushion save that from an area just above it, at about the level of my eyes, there emanated a Voice like the rumble of approaching thunder.

"Willard," said the Voice, "I am becoming a trifle impatient with the way you go around trying to persuade people to speak and write so as to be accurately understood. You are encouraging a mortal sin."

"Surely you don't mean that, Lord."

"Ah, but I do. Let us be logical. Understanding must be based on reason; and since My ways are not to be understood by reason, the foggier people are about Me, the better they and I will get along. Remember the passage from Job: 'Who hath divided a way for the lightning of thunder to cause it to rain on the wilderness, wherein there is no man?' From the point of view of your human understanding, it is nonsense for Me to send the rain upon the wilderness, wherein there is no man. Nonsense and faith, as your writer G. K. Chesterton said so searchingly, are inseparable.

"To be sure, you must pay a price for your lack of understanding—marital squabbles, murders, wars, that sort of thing. But the risks are insignificant by comparison with the principle involved. And besides, it's your own fault—if Adam and Eve hadn't eaten the fruit of that tree, none of these problems would have come up.

"If you recollect, Willard, I gave people a chance at the very start to attain understanding. They all had a single language, and they understood one another perfectly. So what did they do? They used their understanding to build a tower—a ziggurat, rising in tiers, like a wedding cake—which they proposed would reach Heaven itself. If they had succeeded, what would have happened? They would have understood even *Me;* and since I am beyond understanding, they would promptly have gone mad. So I had to limit human understanding to the bare minimum that would give them a chance to keep going. I had to develop jargon."

"How did you accomplish that?"

"I will take you back to Babel," said the Voice, "and you will see for yourself."

I found myself in the midst of a wide plain, gazing on a mound of earth two hundred feet high, with a leveled top. On this foundation thousands of workmen were erecting a tower. The material was brick, and the arrangement was a square, with a ground stage that my eye measured at some two hundred feet to a side. On it stood a second stage, set back from the one below, and on the second a third, and so on, mounting up and up until the ziggurat disappeared into a wreath of fleecy white clouds.

Beside me, also staring at the ziggurat, stood a frail, bearded man in a robe of ass's skin, with glowering eyes; or perhaps it was only the grizzled brows above them that glowered. He was muttering, "I returned, and saw under the sun, that the race is not to the swift, nor the battle to the strong, neither yet bread to the wise, nor yet riches to men of understanding, nor yet favor to men of skill; but time and chance happeneth to them all."

"How close," the Voice whispered, "this mortal has come to understanding the essence of Myself, the Lord his God! This is the road to disaster! But I blind man to his own insights if I simply turn them into jargon. Watch."

The glowering man stopped a passerby and said, "I have a message for you."

"Say on."

"I am the Preacher, and I tell you this: Objective consideration of contemporary phenomena compels the conclusion that success or failure in competitive activities exhibits no tendency to be commensurate with innate capacity, but that a considerable element of the unpredictable must invariably be taken into account."

"Gaa!" said the passerby. He wrenched his arm free and hurried down the street, shaking his head and repeating, "Gaa! Gaa!"

"Could you build a Tower if you received instructions in jargon?" gloated the Voice. "There are two fair young men; let us incapacitate them."

Two bearded youths in a kiln, stripped to the waist, were conversing in undertones as they carefully turned the bottom side of new bricks up to bake to hardness in the burning sun.

"David," said the first, "whatsoever thy soul desireth, I will even do for thee."

"Jonathan, I love thee as my own soul. The Lord be between me and thee, and between my seed and thy seed for ever."

"For these two, a little jargon of the Marin County variety will be the ticket," whispered the Voice. David continued on cue:

"Though I can't say I really dig this Lord-be-between-me-and-thee stuff. Maybe I'm not going with the flow, but somehow I just don't, you know, seem to relate to God."

"Hey, where you coming from, man? God's like laid-back."

"No way. If he's so laid-back, how come he gets so uptight about a little harmless hanky-panky like that serpent-and-apple stuff, right?"

"Right on. Like, wow! Man, you've really *read* the Bible, haven't you?"

"Well, I've flashed on it. But it don't blow my mind."

"Like, the Lord is getting old, you mean. You can't trust a God who's past thirty. These are modern times; we're living in the eleventh chapter of Genesis now, man."*

"Heavy, man. The Lord God just doesn't go with the now."

From the muttering and grumbling in my ear, I gathered that the Lord was not altogether pleased with the comments He had elicited. "Don't worry," I consoled Him; "it's only jargon; it doesn't mean anything. But it's been a revealing experience, Lord. I don't know how you do these things. Is it all right if I get on back to Fifty-first Street now?"

* Somehow David and Jonathan had been transported back in time from the first book of Samuel.

244

"Not quite yet, Willard. Let us see what we can do with the young man and woman discoursing so tenderly there by the well, with the sheep about them."

The young man was saying, "Thine elder sister Leah is tender eyed; but thou, Rachel, art beautiful and well favored. Therefore have I said unto thy father Laban, 'I will serve thee seven years for Rachel thy younger daughter.'"

Rachel replied softly, "With great wrestlings, O my love Jacob, have I wrestled with Leah my sister, and I have prevailed."

A period of smooching ensued, during which the Voice ruminated: "Freudian patter might be the sort of jargon to call on here. Once they get the hang of it, they will spread it all over town."

The couple disentangled themselves, and Jacob said in a troubled tone:

"But Rachel, thou must get back in touch with thy feelings. Leah destroyed thy self-image before thou hadst resolved thine Oedipal crisis, wherefore I fear thou still thinkest adult sexuality a taboo. Thou functionest on a pre-genital level."

"*I?*" exclaimed Rachel indignantly. "*Thou,* Jacob, hast unfulfilled dependency needs, as is known to all thy friends. Dare I wed thee till thou hast overcome them? Wilt thou project thy mother image on me?"

"It is thou who displacest insecurity on *me*, Rachel. Thou thinkest thy father deprived thee of proper parenting; therefore thou compensatest with every man."

"Thou darest so say, who but now accused me of fearing adult sexuality? Am I but a narcissistic extension of thine ego? Even if thy mother spoiled thee, must thou repeat the same syndrome even unto the second and third generation? Thou hast a Madonna-whore model in thine head, Jacob; since I fit not into that fantasy, thou deniest my adult libidinal drives."

At this moment I was approached by a portly gentleman in a loincloth who, as he walked, was scratching with a reed on a roll of papyrus. "Your name, please," he said. "Address. Age. Place of business. Nature of business. Marital status. Annual income. Recent illnesses."

"What is all this about?" I said.

"Royal census, 2247 B.C."

"An ideal subject," murmured the Voice. "Ask him something. Anything."

I said, "How does the Census Bureau make sure that everybody is counted?"

"If more than one area is subject to partial or full suppression no other action within the same area aggregate is necessary. But if only one area is subject to partial suppression then the area with the least number of households (excluding zero) will be subject to partial suppression, unless there is another area at the same area level, with full suppression. Similarly, if only one area is subject to full suppression then the area with the least population but with a number of households greater than zero will be subject to full suppression."

"And how do I decide where my legal domicile is?"

"Your State of Domicile would be the State in which you were born (called 'Domicile of Origin'), unless you had exercised a Domicile of Choice. A Domicile of Choice would be acquired by voluntary determination by yourself to acquire a domicile other than your Domicile of Origin. The personal decision involved would usually be evidenced by a change of residence to the Domicile of Choice, though a change of residence would not in itself indicate a Change of Domicile. The crucial factor in a Change of Domicile is the mental decision that Domicile is Changed. It is implicit in the decision that it is a permanent one; or, to express the matter simply, you have acquired a Domicile of Choice if you have decided to change your Domicile of Origin."

I made my escape by slipping off behind the statue of a fatted calf.

"Lord," I said, "let me go home."

"Only one or two more meetings, Willard," the Voice replied, "and the task will be accomplished."

I found myself in a tent where a tall young lady with raven hair was teaching the Hebrew alphabet to twenty small children seated cross-legged on the floor.

"You are welcome to watch us, sir," she said. "As you will see, ours is a program designed to enhance the concept of open-ended learning with emphasis on a continuum of multiethnic, academically enriched learning using the identified intellectually gifted child as the agent or director of his own learning. Major emphasis is on cross-graded multiethnic learning, with the main objective being to learn respect for the uniqueness of a person. We realize that totally obsolete teaching methods based on imprinting concepts instead of growthful actualizing of potential have created the intellectual ghetto. If schools would stop labeling cooperation 'cheating' and adopt newer methods of student interaction, we wouldn't keep churning out these competitive isolates."

I staggered out.

In another tent two men sat on cushions, dictating to scribes. "They are lawyers," whispered the Voice.

I said to the first man, "Sir, would you mind telling me your legal specialty?"

"I am a divorce lawyer. I brought to Babel the rule that if a man wishes to rid himself of his wife, he must say clearly: 'I divorce thee, I divorce thee, I divorce thee.'"

"Too simple," whispered the Voice. "Ask him another question, and I'll turn on the jargon."

"What if the husband changes his mind afterward?"

The lawyer tugged at his nose, stroked his beard, and replied, "Ah, sir, he should bear in mind that there should be a finality to litigation; all types of evils can arise from a situation in which a party obtains its own independent counsel, such counsel presents the documents to the Court and the same are approved by the Court and made a part of the final decree and thereafter the party who initiated such divorce action and sought such counsel and had the same presented to the Court challenges such agreement of the parties that became part of the final decree and thereafter the party who initiated such divorce action and sought such counsel and had the same presented to the Court challenges such agreement of the parties that became part of the divorce agreement, no matter what the grounds of that challenge might be."

I turned to the second lawyer. "Sir," I said, "my home is in a country where we grow a delicious fruit known as an orange. Suppose I am an orange grower, and generally sell my produce, but am moved to make a friend a gift of an orange. If I simply say, 'I give you this orange,' am I legally bound?"

He replied instantly, "My dear fellow! The gift would have no legal validity whatever. The recipient could not even sniff the fragrance of the fruit without risking a suit for damages. No, the transfer must be in the form of a written document, stating: 'Know all men by these presents that I hereby give, grant, bargain, sell, release, convey, transfer, and quit-claim all my right, title, interest, benefit, and use whatever in, of, and concerning this chattel, otherwise known as an orange, or *Citrus aurantium*, together with all the appurtenances thereto of skin, pulp, pip, rind, seeds, and juice, to have and to hold the said orange together with its skin, pulp, pip, rind, seeds, and juice for his own use and behoof, to himself and his heirs in fee simple forever, free from all liens, encumbrances, easements, limitations, restraints, or conditions whatsoever, any and all prior deeds, transfers or other documents whatsoever, now or anywhere made, to the contrary notwithstanding, with full power to bite, cut, suck, or otherwise eat the said orange or to give away the same, with or without its skin, pulp, pip, rind, seeds, or juice.' "

There was a snort of suppressed laughter in my ear. "He said all that," whispered the Voice, "before I had even had a chance to put a whammy on him!"

"By the time God had finished putting jargon into the mouths of the people of Babel," I told F.D.R., "the worshipers could not understand their priests, the children could not understand their teachers, the lovers could not understand each other. Within hours there was internecine fighting all over the ziggurat. Within days the Tower collapsed; no more was left of it than remains of Ozymandias, king of kings."

"But that was four thousand years ago," said Roosevelt. "What is God worrying about now?"

"Mr. President, every time someone splits a gene or an atom, or, for that matter, creates a symphony or a *Last Supper,* God sees it as a brick in a new Tower. And He is already taking his countermeasures—turning languages back into regional dialects, and dialects into jargon and gibberish."

"I won't have it," said Roosevelt. "The American people won't have it. You just watch, Willard. I am going to call for a new election in Heaven. I am going to put together a collection of angels, and ethnics, and blue-collar workers, and intellectuals, and afflicted minorities. And oh, yes—cherubim. Don't look skeptical—we have nothing to fear but fear itself. We are going to

throw out that reactionary old Herbert Hoover of a Je-
hovah."

("Watch yourself, Willard," warned the Voice in my
ear. "It's a good time for you to stay neutral, my boy."

("God," I said fervently, "you can count on that.")

APPENDIX:
Authors or Sources of
Jargon Used:

The Lord's Prayer: Ivor Brown and James B. Minor
Ecclesiastes: George Orwell
Psychobabble: Cyra McFadden
Psychiatry: Freudian terminology
Census Bureau: British Census Office, Irish accounting
house
Education: Richard Mitchell, others
Legalese: Richard H. Mundheim, Ronald Goldfarb

FOR EVERY WORD ALIVE,
A SPECIAL STORY

For every word alive, a special story;
  For every story, its own special joy.
What sport that sorrow *is no kin to* sorry!
  What fun that girl *once meant the same as* boy!

Spade up Old English sorg, *the root of* sorrow—
  Two one in meaning, neither less nor more.
But sorry's *a coincidental borrow*
  From Anglo-Saxon sarig, *meaning "sore."*

A Middle English child of either sex
  Was gurle—*that is, "a person still ungrown."*
(Ah, lucky gurles—*with life still uncomplex,*
  With Women's Liberation still unknown!)

Friend, grumble not that life is reft of glory,
  That all conspires to fuddle and annoy,
As long as sorrow *is no kin to* sorry—
  As long as girl *once meant the same as* boy!

FAREWELL TO THE HOUSE ON FIFTY-FIRST STREET

THOUGH real estate has been booming in Manhattan, the house on Fifty-first Street—the physical house, that is—stayed on the market for more than a score of years. Day after day I would walk past it, and read the fading sign attached to the wrought-iron fence: "INTERESTED PARTIES MAY ARRANGE AN INSPECTION BY CALLING 752-2309." Occasionally I would check with the bank handling the estate of the former owners, and they would report that there were still no bids. Potential buyers, they said, would look through the house and come away with an uncomfortable feeling that the place was haunted. I could not fault them, since it is I who do the haunting.

But what would happen, I wondered, if someone *did* buy the brownstone that houses my brain?

The question became more than academic last summer, when photographers began to take pictures of fashion models with 479 East Fifty-first Street as a background. When fashion models pose before a building, that building is *in*. Later, the city affixed a brass plaque to the fence, saying, "BECAUSE OF THE ARCHITECTURAL SIGNIFICANCE OF THIS RESIDENCE, ERECTED IN 1910, IT HAS BEEN PLACED ON THE ROSTER OF OFFICIAL LANDMARKS BY THE BOROUGH OF MANHATTAN."

To label a New York brownstone a landmark is to say that it is about to be replaced by a high-rise apartment house or office building. So I was not surprised last week to see that a wooden fence with holes in it for spying had been set up along the sidewalk, while a gargantuan crane, dangling an ominous wrecking ball, was locked into position on the street. The bank confirmed that the house on Fifty-first Street had been acquired by a consortium, and that demolition would begin the following Monday, which was yesterday.

The fate of my brain is of considerable concern to me, so I made a point of being in the house by nine in the morning. Something was going on outside, all right; men shouted, whistles whistled, machinery clanked. I did not look; I waited. But not for long. At nine thirty-five A.M. exactly, the wrecking ball (after, I presume, a few preliminary waggles) came smashing into my sanctuary.

Or so, at least, it must have seemed to the operator of the crane, and the idlers who had paused to watch. In their eyes, no doubt, the walls crumpled one by one, until finally the entire brownstone tumbled down. Yet to me, sitting at my desk, the house remained undisturbed; the wrecking ball was only a wraith, of no more consequence to my life than are clouds to the sun which they momentarily obscure.

Tomorrow, when I pass on the sidewalk, I shall be able to look through the spy holes in the fence and see the rubble of the house on Fifty-first Street being scooped away. Someday soon an office building will stand there. But it makes no difference. The brownstone that houses my brain remains as before, and I shall enjoy it undisturbed. I shall continue to entertain my guests from other times. My only regret is that you, my living friends, cannot come calling.